How Families Flourish

A Character Building Guide for Developing a Strength Based Family using Positive Psychology

Daniel Trussell, Ph.D.

Notes to Readers

While the scenarios and stories in this book come from real life, names and distinguishing characteristics have been omitted to assure confidentiality is protected.

The ideas, techniques, interventions and processes in this book are not intended as a substitute for the treatment of mental health problems. Consult with a mental health professional if you are experiencing mental health problems before using the techniques described in this book.

> How Families Flourish: A Character Building Guide for Developing a Strengths Based Family using Positive Psychology
>
> ISBN-13 978-1479105526
>
> ISBN-10 147910552X
>
> Library of Congress Control Number   2012914883

Copyright © 2012 by Daniel Trussell, Ph.D. Alpharetta, Georgia. All rights reserved. No part of this book may be reproduced in any form whatsoever without written consent from the author. The author can be contacted at daniel@howfamiliesflourish.com

Table of Contents

Is Your Family Flourishing or Floundering? 1
How to Foster a Flourishing Family 1
   Promote good self-esteem and well-being 1
   Communicate respectfully 4
   Manage anger 10
   Determine the meaning and purpose of your family 12
   Get the family more engaged with each other 15
   Embrace an optimistic mindset 18
   Deepen resiliency 21
   What you think is how you feel and behave – the ABCs 24
   Learn to avoid automatic thinking 36
   Extinguish learned helplessness and replace it with mastery 39
   Practice calming and focusing strategies 47
   Teach Self Determination 50
   Increase family vitality 53
   Extend Positive Relationships 57
   Generate more positive emotions in your family 61
   Forgive others and don't hold grudges 67
   Confront a crisis head-on 71
   Put the outcome in perspective 74
   Seven mistakes floundering parents make 76
   Determining virtues and strengths –the work begins 85
   Talents versus strengths 89

Internally validate your core strengths 92
Lifting barriers to accessing our core strengths 95
The Strengths defined 97
Wisdom – acquiring and using knowledge... 97
    Love of Learning 97
    Judgment 100
    Curiosity 102
    Originality 106
    Perspective 109
Courage – accomplishing goals in the face of opposition 111
    Integrity 112
    Bravery... 115
    Persistence 119
    Vitality 125
Humanity and Love – strengths of befriending and tending to others
.... 131
    Generosity 131
    Loving and Being Loved 136
    Social/Emotional Intelligence 141
Justice – strengths that build community 146
    Teamwork 146
    Fairness.. 150
    Leadership... 154
Temperance – strengths that protect against excess 157
    Forgiveness and Mercy 157
    Self Control.. 161

- Humility 166
- Prudence and Discretion 169
- Transcendence – strengths that connect us to the larger universe 173
  - Appreciation 173
  - Gratitude 176
  - Hope 180
  - Spirituality 184
  - Humor 187
- Bringing it together 189

The Family Charter 193
- What is a Family Charter? 194
- How to write a mission statement 196
- Family Rules 198
- Consequences 211
- Rewards 218
  - Allowances 226
- Chores 227
- Putting It All Together 232
- Revealing your Family Charter 236

Preface

How Families Flourish is a compilation of over sixty years of research from brilliant social scientists who posited theories, conducted laboratory studies and pushed their findings into real world applications. I take no credit for developing any individual theories or techniques reported in this book, although I have combined them into a unique program.

As a positive psychology family coach and professional counselor, I take the insights of others and provide a structure and experience that can be internalized with the families and agencies with whom I work. All the techniques, processes and information in this book are evidence based. Evidence based or best practices are processes and programs that have been used repeatedly with a similar outcome and reported in scientific literature. To qualify as an evidence based practice, the process or program is rigorously studied in real life applications to determine if similar outcomes are obtained. An evidence based practice has a rigid definition of rules of practice. It has been shown that the further one strays from the prescribed activities, the less likely participants will have an outcome similar to participants in the studies.

While How Families Flourish is derivative in that it identifies and defines the concepts and outcomes of researchers; it is original in its structural components and combines multiple evidence based practices into a framework that is easy to use.

Acknowledgements I have read literally thousands of scholarly articles and books over the last thirty five years to develop this program and it would be impossible to cite them all. Therefore I have boldly chosen not to annotate this book, much to the chagrin of my professional colleagues. Instead, I urge the reader to do her own research on topics of interest.

www.wikipedia.com is an excellent resource on Positive Psychology and the contributors to those articles accurately represent what journals and books on Positive Psychology report. I have listed below the major researchers and theorists referred to in the text by order of appearance in the body of the book. No doubt, I have missed many other significant contributors to the development of this program. This is by no means a comprehensive list, just a starting point for your own journey.

Corey Keyes, Ph.D.

Mihaly Csikszentmihalyi, Ph.D.

Martin Seligman, Ph.D.

Ellen Langer, Ph.D.

Edward Thorndike, Ph.D.

Albert Ellis, Ph.D.

Aaron Beck, Ph.D.

Barbara Fredrickson, Ph.D.

Abraham Maslow, Ph.D.

Neal Miller, Ph.D.

John Dollard, Ph.D.

Albert Bandura, Ph.D.

Alex Linley, Ph.D.

Mary Ainsworth, Ph.D.

Lawrence Kohlberg, Ph.D.

Carol Gilligan, Ph.D.

Robert Enright, Ph.D.

Charles Carver, Ph.D.

Michael Scheier, Ph.D.

Charles Snyder, Ph.D.

Sigmund Freud, M.D.

Jane Gillham, Ph.D.

Karen Reivich, Ph.D.

Matthew Johnson, Psy.D.

B.F. Skinner, Ph.D.

I also want to acknowledge the families who have given me the opportunity to put the program into practice. Without you, this book could never have been written.

Major fields of study that contributed to this work include

Psychoanalytic theory

Behavior theory

Behavior Modification

Operant Conditioning

Cognitive therapy

Rational Emotive therapy

Cognitive Behavioral therapy

Dialectical Behavioral therapy

Positive Psychology

Attachment theory

Broaden and build theory

Social learning theory

Social action theory

Moral development theory

Flow

Flourishing

Positive Discipline

I want to express gratitude to the following people for their assistance in editing and enhancing this book.

> Tim Browning, IT Consultant, Kimberly Clark, Alpharetta, Georgia
>
> Darlene Cook, Early Childhood Trainer & Consultant, Lynnwood, Washington

Introduction

This book is divided into three distinction sections with specific skills and objectives for each section. Combined, they become a powerful program for improving well-being, positive emotions, optimism, flow and flourishing for your family. Section One, How to Foster a Flourishing Family, provides eighteen ways to improve household harmony and seven behaviors to avoid disrupting that harmony.

Section Two, Strength based living, describes the twenty four character strengths identified in Positive Psychology to build resilience to life's challenges, broaden positive emotional experience and increase life satisfaction. Not all strengths are available to young children because of the developmental stage in which they reside. Indeed, the character strength humor doesn't fully develop until the late teens, although young children can be quite amusing. The character strength forgiveness matures as we do. Young children are the least forgiving (without the element of revenge or restitution) and seniors the most forgiving. The unique beauty of identifying and accessing core strengths (the strengths you most closely align with) is that it is not pathologically based. Rather than fixing problems and trying to be what you are not, using core strengths allows each member of the family to be the best they can be and to celebrate their talents, skills and strengths and determine how those contribute to the flourishing family.

Section Three, The Family Charter is a practical guide to setting the stage for every family to experience security, consistency and integrity in their home. Topics include developing a Family Mission Statement, family rules, and the consequences when rules are broken, how to develop a meaningful reward system and assigning family chores. Scores of families tell me that the Family

Charter transformed and reinvigorated their stagnant households. Even if you don't take the time to produce a physical Family Charter, this section includes valuable information about what to think about if you want an orderly household that supports the flourishing family.

While this program is valuable for all age children and their parents, it is especially suited for families with ten to thirteen year olds living in the household. By the age of ten, children have reached the developmental stage where they can grasp and experience all the concepts in this program. If you have a question or comment, you can email me at Daniel@howfamiliesflourish.com. I hope to hear from you!

Is Your Family Flourishing or Floundering?

What percentage of the time does your family share positive emotions when you are all together? Some families are in such a rush to get tasks accomplished that there is little time devoted to cultivating an environment where everyone thrives. Ask yourself the following questions.

Does our family frequently engage in activities together that every member of the family enthusiastically participates in and looks forward to?

Does our family pursue a shared vision, meaning or purpose?

Does every member of our family have good self-esteem, a sense of well-being and experience an abundance of positive emotions

Do we generally feel positive about other members of our family?

Is our family optimistic about the future of the family? Do we share this optimism with each other?

Does our family bounce back quickly when things go wrong or we face adversity?

Do the members of our family spontaneously express that they really care about each other and look forward to spending time together as a family unit?

If you answered yes to all the questions, you have created an environment where your family has the opportunity to flourish. Flourishing is a concept founded in the field of positive psychology. Positive psychology is distinct from other fields of psychology in that it seeks to focus on the presence or absence of positive traits and determines evidence based methods of building positive emotional experience. Positive Psychology also conducts research to determine ways to prevent mental illness. Authentic happiness and well-being theory are part of the positive psychology movement along with creating flow and resiliency.

The questions you answered above are related to the core and additional elements found in people who are flourishing. Core features found in people who are flourishing include

- positive emotions
- engagement and interest
- meaning and purpose

Additional components seen in people who are flourishing are

- good self-esteem and well-being
- optimism
- resilience
- vitality
- self determination
- positive relationships

Dr. Corey Keyes, a sociologist and one of the founders of the positive psychology movement, and many other academicians, study traits of persons whom Keyes describes as either flourishing or languishing. Based on the evidence, a growing number of helping professionals think that there is a difference between a person who is depressed and one who is languishing although from a psychopathologist's point of view the two may seem indistinguishable. Research supports that languishing can contribute to episodes of depression, anxiety or other mental health problems.

Flourishing people, estimated at about a third of the population, exhibit higher levels of emotional well-being and have high life satisfaction. Flourishing people have purpose and meaning in their lives, are self-accepting and are accepting of others as well. They participate in social and community activities and are in a state of actualizing their lives and assisting others in doing the same.

People floundering, or as Keyes calls it languishing, tend to have low emotional and social well-being. There is a sense of emptiness and suffering, often accompanied by avoidance of social activities. Floundering people may also seek out frequent achievement recognition as validation that they are worthwhile individuals. They are, for the most part, disengaged from others and their community.

Another distinction between flourishing people and floundering people is how they experience flow, a concept studied by Dr. Mihaly Csikszentmihalyi. Flourishing people know flow; languishing people have low flow. The science of flow is an entire body of work but very briefly it could be described as that time when someone is so fully challenged by and engaged in a task that distractions, and time itself, fall aside. It is a time of full engagement but does not produce anxiety or a fear of failing if something doesn't go right.

For example, I am an avid gardener and especially like germinating seeds in winter to plant in my garden in the spring. Last year, I grew over 2000 plants from seeds! When I am concocting the planting mix, filling the pots, handling and planting each seed, placing the trays under the grow lights, watering, watching life spring forth, transplanting seedlings to larger pots, planting the plants in the garden and taking an evening stroll through the garden, I lose track of all time. I am fully present but lose my sense of individual self. While I know all the seeds won't germinate and all the seedlings won't survive, I am undeterred. I feel joy and hope. I add value to my neighborhood by increasing its beauty and others appreciation of nature as they take their evening walk through the neighborhood. However, when I have to drag out the garden hose and water those plants outdoors on a hot day, the only thing flowing is the water through the hose.

A number of research findings demonstrate that people who are languishing in a pessimistic world view without avenues of connecting to flow have lower self-esteem, more persistent and chronic illness and higher absentee rates at work or school than those who are more optimistic and flourishing in life. It has also been found that pessimistic and depressed people have about an equal number of positive and negative thoughts whereas flourishing or optimistic people have twice as many positive thoughts about themselves, others and the world in which they live. Positive psychology is scientifically proven to build and broaden happiness and teach people how to create a life more worth living. Positive psychology seeks to improve one's permanent well-being through a variety of techniques.

Dr. Martin Seligman talks about the need to look at ways to change one's explanation about the world, called explanatory styles, from pessimistic to optimistic. He advocates that people identify their strengths and find ways to demonstrate those strengths in the world. I'll show you ways to change your explanatory style from pessimistic to optimistic and help you identify strengths for each of your family members and use them to increase your family's life satisfaction later in the book.

Just as individuals, families also flounder or flourish, based on the household environment, family attitudes and the world view of the family members. If your family is floundering, it's time to change your family's thoughts and behaviors. By applying the tools you learn throughout this book, your family will learn how to move into a world full of optimism, resilience and flow. You'll learn how to elicit more positive emotions in the household and how to help your children build character, handle life's challenges with grace, experience more pride in their accomplishments and improve communication within the family. The following sections will introduce you to the basic goals your family will learn to master as they become a more fully flourishing family.

How to Foster a Flourishing Family

How to Foster a Flourishing Family

Promote good self-esteem and well-being

Every individual is responsible for their own level of self-esteem and building good self-esteem. How your child maintains good self-esteem requires continual monitoring on the part of the child. Parents can, however, do much to help a child with low self-esteem move toward good self-esteem. Conversely, high self-esteem can be confronted and replaced with good self-esteem. There is an abundance of articles, exercises, books and workshops on how to build good self-esteem. I think a more important focus for the family is building well-being. When your child lives in a state of well-being, good self-esteem is a natural byproduct.

When we emphasize building or correcting self-esteem, our goal is to fix a problem. Positive psychology helps people move beyond correcting defects and managing symptoms of low or high self-esteem. Dr. Martin Seligman identified five pillars of well-being and developed the acronym PERMA to describe those pillars.

Positive Emotion

Engagement

Relationship

Meaning

Accomplishment

Examples of **positive emotions** include joy, gratitude, peace, love, pleasure, curiosity, inspiration and hope. Positive emotions are reinforced when your child draws upon her signature strengths, talents and abilities. Positive emotions are increased when your child engages in acts of kindness and selflessness.

Engagement can be taught to you child by helping her identify activities such as hobbies or sports or civic involvement that really matter to her and that she is genuinely enthusiastic about. Making your child play piano when all she wants to do is play soccer can lead to disengagement. Engagement leads to the state of flow discussed later in this chapter.

Maintaining meaningful and satisfying **relationships** with peers, family and other adults will increase optimism. Encourage your children to seek out meaningful relationships. It is not the number of friends your child has but the quality of those relationships that builds optimism.

Meaning and purpose in your child's life may seem ambitious, especially if you have very young children. Meaning in life comes about when we realize we align with a cause that is bigger than ourselves. Help your child identify causes she believes in and support her participation. Sometimes belonging to a school spirit team, a sports team or an after school club helps a child find meaning in her life. Contributing to family harmony is a cause bigger than the individuals in the family.

Celebrate your child's **accomplishments** and achievements. Ask how she feels when she has tackled a project that is challenging. Offer a privilege such as an outing with you to the park, zoo or event she wants to attend as an achievement reward.

Dr. Ellen Langer has demonstrated that people become optimistic and experience more happiness, and thus a boost to well-being, when they are GLADO.

Generous – such as forgiving, offering to help

Loving – to self and others

Authentic – being the real you

Direct – asking for what you want, saying no

Open – to new experience and interpretations, flexibility

Helping your child pay attention to the here and now experience of these characteristics and behaviors builds positive emotional experience and nurtures good self-esteem.

Communicate respectfully

The way we communicate, both verbally and non-verbally, impacts outcomes and family dynamics every day. Teach your child how to be assertive, not passive or aggressive when he wants to get his point across or when he has a request of you or needs to say no to someone. We want our children to stand up for themselves and be self-confident. We want our children to learn how to not be bullied or manipulated.

Assertive communication respects the boundaries of others while giving your child the opportunity to protect his own boundaries. Assertive communication allows your child to express feelings and desires directly, without triggering aggression. People who are assertive are able to freely express their thoughts, feelings and needs. They have control over their anger. They are willing to compromise, taking the needs and desires of others into consideration, as long as they don't feel violated by the compromise.

Aggressive communication is ineffective and leads to a child feeling judged or threatened which can escalate to verbal or physical assaults. Parents who excessively criticize, belittle or shout at their children teach children a set of skills that will not help them in the long run and reduce their child's capacity to have meaningful and satisfying relationships. Children who communicate aggressively may sometime get immediate gratification but it is short lived and not very satisfying. Aggressive communication does little to improve self-esteem or well-being.

Passive communication allows others to violate your child's personal boundaries and leads your child to playing the role of a victim, helpless to change things. Even if the child lashes out later at the offending party, it is driven by anger and becomes an aggressive communication style. In either case it does not help your child feel in control of his life and have mastery over his environment.

Several assertive techniques can be taught to your child. Let your child know they do not have to be either a victim or a bully because being assertive is a better way to communicate. Four techniques you can introduce to your child:

> **Use I statements**. Here is a simple sentence map to teach your child to use. "When you _____ (the behavior or action), I think or feel _____ (identify thought or feeling) and I want or need _____ (what your child wants different from what she got). For example, your child tells

you she is hurt with her best friend because her friend did not invite her to a sleepover. You help her practice the "I statement" that she can then use with her friend such as "When you don't invite me to your parties, I feel angry and hurt (sad) and it damages our friendship. I hope you will invite me to your next party."

Don't agree, but ask for more specific information. Teach your child that he doesn't have to agree on anything the moment it is presented to him. Help him learn that if he doesn't want to do something or he wants someone to do something they don't want to do, he can gather more information and decide at a later time. Help your child understand she has the right to disagree, even with you. It may not change your opinion or request, but you are acknowledging that your child has a viewpoint and you want to know what it is. This technique teaches your child to think things through instead of acting impulsively or giving in to pressure from peers. Finally, this technique instills self-determination in your child.

Agree to disagree. Find the points you can agree with but remain firm in your position. Your child has recently purchased a black and white e book reader and wants you to upgrade her to a full color version. She promises she will read more, take better care of it and describes the technology differences to you. You reply "While I agree it is more technologically advanced, and you might read more, I don't think you would take better care of a color reader than the one you have. Your reader is still new so the answer is no."

Repeat your request again and again (broken record). You child can learn to repeat a request, or refuse a request from another each time there is resistance to her position. While this is the easiest assertive technique to teach one's child, it is met with the most resistance by parents. Parents fear their child will try to use it against them. The techniques you can use so this doesn't backfire on you include

- making it a family rule that broken record is not allowed from child to parent
- call your child on it and let them know this is manipulation, not assertion

- continue saying no, or insisting on your request, and walk away from further discussion

Every parent needs to reinforce these simple assertive tools when peers pressure your child to use drugs or alcohol, break the law or engage in sexual activities or unsafe sex (when your child is thinking about becoming sexually active).

Let's look at a scenario to review the three possible styles of communication. Your child goes to the mall with two friends every Saturday. The other two girls have each stolen a small cosmetic item but your child has not participated despite strong peer pressure. Now her friends are badgering her to become a member of the "shoplift club" and tell her she must steal an item this Saturday to prove her loyalty to them. She comes to you for advice. You have three possible responses.

Passive: "I wouldn't worry about it; they will eventually stop asking you to steal something if you don't shoplift this Saturday."

Result: Doesn't fix the problem.

Aggressive: "I'll put a stop to this. I'm calling their mothers and you won't have anything to do with them again"

Result: Child feels she has betrayed her friends and loses trust in family confidentiality.

Assertive: You help your child construct an assertive response such as "I don't want to play this game. It is against the law and one of our family rules is to never steal. I feel frustrated that you keep asking me to play your game and I don't want you to ask me to participate ever again"

Result: Your child set clear limits, refused to have boundaries violated and stood her ground. You as a parent may indeed want your child to stop going to the mall with these friends or feel compelled to tell their parents what they have done. If this is the case, how would you handle it assertively, without violating the trust your child has in you?

You might help your child build an additional assertive statement to say to her friends. "I talked about this with my parents and they told me I have to stop going to the mall with you. I feel sad that I can't keep going out with you on Saturday. My parents think your parents need to know what you have done but they agree that they will give you a chance to tell them yourselves first. I am sorry I put you in this position but I can't change it."

Manage anger

Anger is good. You read that right. Anger is good and a necessary feeling state for all human beings. Anger is a strong motivator, a protective shield and a catalyst for the expression of feelings. Without anger, social change is unlikely. People don't end up in a protest march because they are happy with the way things are. They protest because the anger they feel about a cause is a call to action for them. People express hurt, frustration or disappointment because they are angry. The expression of anger is a warning to others to "back off" because you are feeling violated or threatened. Anger can help you feel more in control of a situation, even if you have no control over the situation. There are ways to express anger that are inappropriate and parents need to teach their children that, while anger is going to happen to every person, some behaviors associated with the feeling of anger are unacceptable.

Humans express four basic feeling states: Mad, glad, sad and scared. These feeling states are programmed into us and we feel all four of them, based on environmental, behavioral or thought triggers. We can't avoid experiencing anger, happiness, sadness or fear. Nonetheless, we spend a lot of energy trying to avoid the things that frighten us or make us sad. We chase after happiness, often in destructive or nonsensical ways. We try to suppress or deny our anger for fear of losing control.

Trying to teach your child not to get angry is trying to teach your child to not feel. As long as a person is alive, the mind is hardwired to identify and express the basic four feelings of mad, glad, sad and scared. Spend time teaching your child to identify anger, acknowledge it, listen to what it is telling her, and harness it so she can engage in problem solving to reduce the anger provoking thought or behavior. Anger is a problem if it is too frequent, if it lasts too long or if it leads to aggression. Frequent out of control anger or rage can lead to health problems and stress the heart or dangerously raise blood pressure. Taking anger out on others is also a problem.

As parents you teach your children about using expressions of anger appropriately by modeling that behavior for them. Don't be threatened by your child's anger. Let them know there are consequences for expressing anger inappropriately. In the section titled Family Charter, I'll show you how to use Character Cards (an assignment, typically additional chores) to shape appropriate behavior. One family rule you might want to have is that inappropriate expressions of anger will result in drawing from the Character Card deck.

When you child gets angry, it is an opportunity to demonstrate respect for his feelings, encourage his problem solving skills, teach conflict resolution strategies and model empathy. Empathic responses such as "I understand you are angry but I won't fix this problem for you", lead to better problem solving skills on your child's part.

You want to share your anger with your child when there is a legitimate reason to be angry with her but not when you are angry because she was not perfect or you become impatient with her. Nor is it appropriate for you to express anger toward your child because you selfishly want something but the family needs supersede your individual desire. Finally, refuse to express anger toward your child because of your own petty preferences such as "I'm mad at you because you chose the yellow blouse over the pink blouse and the pink blouse was so much cuter."

Determine the meaning and purpose of your family

Later in this book you will be challenged to write a Mission Statement, the preamble to your Family Charter. A Family Charter is a document that includes family rules, consequences for breaking those rules, a rewards system and a list of chores assigned to each family member. The Mission Statement is a powerful acknowledgement of the meaning and purpose of your family. The Mission Statement declares that there is a cause bigger than the individual members that call themselves a family and that by agreeing to follow the Family Charter each individual contributes to the greater good of the family.

Flourishing families also find individual ways to have meaning for their lives outside the family. For instance, you may be deeply invested in volunteering at a homeless shelter soup kitchen and want your family to know the satisfaction you get when giving back to the community. Once a month the entire family volunteers as a way to show the children the value of civic involvement and help them build meaning in their lives. Two of your children talk about how good it feels to volunteer and get up early to get to the soup kitchen at least 15 minutes before their shift. Your third child has to be reminded repeatedly that it's time to go. While he also talks about how good it feels to participate in this service to the community, you notice he routinely is not very enthusiastic during the shift. These are signals that your third child may not see this as an activity that brings meaning into his life and he is just participating because the family expects it.

Do you know what your child is really passionate about? Careful observation will help you learn. The illustration above simply demonstrates that no one can choose for another person what brings meaning into a person's life. Nonetheless there are ways to support your children in identifying what will bring meaning into their lives. When looking at a cause that is bigger than ourselves, consider that evidence suggests that the larger the entity to which we affiliate, the more meaning we can derive from being a part of that group.

Why is meaning so important to a family? Finding a meaning or purpose allows us to give up personal control and concern for self. It allows us to put the well-being of others over our own individual well-being. One way for your child to experience this is to teach your child how to give things away to those in need. You might want to try this exercise.

Tell your child he has 2 days to determine which toy, article of clothing, book, game, $5.00 of cash he has saved or reward tokens (you'll learn about those in the Family Charter section of the book) that he is going to give someone that needs it more than he needs it. Your child doesn't have to like this exercise and he doesn't have to choose his most prized possession.

During those two days, help your child identify who he is going to give the gift to. If he has trouble coming up with a recipient you can offer examples. Some examples might include giving to a child his age who lost everything in a local fire, someone he knows who has lost a family member and is mourning, a relief effort following a natural disaster or a family at church or in the local neighborhood who has fallen on hard times. While the most powerful learning experience will come from your child actually giving the selected item directly to the recipient, that is not always practical. You may have to help him mail it somewhere but you should let him stand in line at the post office and complete the transaction. The more personally involved he is the more meaning it will have for him. Dropping an old pair of jeans that no longer fit in a charity box to be given to an anonymous recipient will have the smallest beneficial effect.

I've worked with many families who repeat this exercise every month. Study after study has shown that doing things for others as a purposeful action increases happiness and life satisfaction. A life with meaning simply means finding something worth living for.

Get the family more engaged with each other

With the hectic lives most families lead, getting your family more connected may seem to you to be the most challenging of all the tools to help your family flourish. But engagement is not about the amount of time you spend together but what happens when you spend time together. Between homework, shopping, school, work and after school activities it may be difficult for your family to even get together every night for dinner. Even when you do get together, it may be hard to keep your family members' attention for very long. In many families, people talk to each other and not with each other. Flourishing families have to work hard to make family time sacred and primary to family life. I challenge you to devote one hour a week at the same time every week where everyone is in the same room at the same time for a regularly scheduled family meeting.

The family meeting is a time to celebrate victories together, to problem solve family challenges and to make plans for the future. It's a time to model optimism, respectful communication and conflict resolution in an open and safe environment. It demonstrates commitment from all family members that they appreciate being a part of the family, are grateful to have an opportunity to get together and willing to give up personal time for the higher cause of the family.

Regularly scheduled family meetings can be awkward at first as the family is faced with an uncharted territory. It's easy to have some important event to one family member come up and the family is requested to reschedule the meeting to another time. Don't! Even one violation gives way to eroding the importance of the meeting. The section on Family Charter will give you additional pointers about the family meeting.

For engagement to take place during a family meting several elements must be present. Each person must have a willingness to solve problems during the meeting. Family meetings start and end promptly. If the problem isn't solved by the end of the meeting, it is put on the agenda for review at the next week's meeting. This gives each family member time to reflect on the barriers to solving a problem and construct possible solutions. A second element is to identify and utilize individual and family strengths and to stay focused on activities that reinforce those strengths. Strengths will be discussed in detail in the Strength based living section of this book.

The third element that must be present is understanding the importance of your family norms. Family norms are principles of correct action that serves to guide, control or regulate proper and acceptable behavior within the family. Likely, if you are a two parent household your family norms are a combination of both of your family of origin norms and that make sense to both parents to continue to live by. Examples of family norms are going to religious service regularly, having dinner together every night, saying grace or a blessing at meals, everyone gets a birthday cake every year, at least one parent attends school events like a play or sporting events, going to Grandma's house for thanksgiving dinner, no dating before age sixteen. Unlike family rules where there is an identified consequence if you break a rule, family norms are the kinds of values, activities and beliefs that your family presumes to share in common. Children typically bring the family norms of their parents into adulthood and teach them to their children.

Family norms are not typically open for discussion in family meetings but may be brought up at other times the family is talking. For example, your child says to you during a family meeting that all her friends are dating at 13 and she can't see why she has to wait until she is 16. It's a given, a norm, that your children will not date until they are 16. This would not be a productive use of time during the family meeting although you could talk about your reasons for this norm at another time.

Embrace an optimistic mindset

Essential to a flourishing family is the mindset of optimism. In a culture dominated with pessimism, teaching your child how to become optimistic may seem to be a daunting task. Evidence show that adopting an optimistic world view leads to improved health, increased achievement and better control of mood and well-being. Optimism is a relatively easy concept to teach and grasp.

What sets optimists apart from pessimists is the way in which they view the victories and setbacks in their lives. Optimists think that a setback is temporary while pessimists see a setback (failure, defeat, not getting what you wanted or thought you needed) as more permanent.

Your child seems really excited about being a cheerleader and has been practicing all year. She attended cheerleading camp and practiced every day. She tries out for the cheerleading squad in the 9th grade but is not selected. If she is an optimist she sees this as an opportunity to practice her skills, get better at it and try out again next year. If she is a pessimist, she likely engages in negative self-talk ("I'm a failure", "I'll never be good enough") that leads to her giving up, not practicing for next year's tryouts and moving on to a different interest.

Regarding victories, an optimist thinks that a victory lasts forever and builds on well-being while a pessimist thinks that a victory is situation specific, won't last and fails to give herself credit for making the victory happen. Let's use the scenario above only this time your child was selected to be on the team.

If she is an optimist she might think "Wow! All that hard work really paid off. I'm only in the 9th grade so I have plenty of time to get better and better every year." If she is a pessimist she might think "They just had to pick a 9th grader and only three of us tried out. It's just a lucky break, but I'll probably get cut during the season because the other cheerleaders are older and have a lot more experience. I'd better not get too excited about being selected."

Other tools to help your child become an optimist are helping your child identify what he is grateful for, teaching about how to forgive, teaching how to recognize and acknowledge when he is in a state of deep appreciation and nurturing his core strengths.

To learn how to identify and express gratitude takes no more than 3 minutes a day. Before your child goes to bed at night have her list 3 things she was grateful for today. If she practices this nighttime ritual every day, within a few weeks she will start doing this naturally throughout the day and probably make it a lifelong habit.

A third difference between optimists and pessimists, and the subject of the next section, is how quickly they bounce back from adversity. This is known as resilience. Optimists believe "I can change it" while pessimists believe "This is going to last forever."

Deepen resiliency

Resilience is being able to bounce back from an offsetting experience. People who are resilient don't get overwhelmed by doubt or shy away from challenges. Resilient people don't feel shame when they don't succeed at a challenge they have taken on. They learn from a failure and affix meaning to that failure. Failure is not an endpoint for resilient people.

Resiliency is not innate and must be learned. Some learn it more naturally than others but everyone can learn the skill set. Resilience is not a personality trait but a way one thinks about things. Self-criticism lessens one's ability to become resilient. Failure at one activity that is generalized from "I failed my math test" to "I am a failure" leads to helplessness and, ultimately, hopelessness. One technique to help overcome destructive self-criticism is to teach your children that being self-critical for a particular failing is an opportunity for reflection and problem solving.

Likewise, blaming others for what we experience is equally toxic to resiliency. "It's my math teacher's fault I failed my math test. She just doesn't like me." Help your child recognize that this is an opportunity to determine how he contributed to the failure by changing his viewpoint to something like "My math teacher expects us to understand something the first time she introduces it. If I don't understand something in the future, I will ask her to explain it to me again."

How do we teach our children to frame failure or disappointment as an opportunity to develop a more resilient response to life's challenges? Teaching a child to overcome negative thinking, helping them become more flexible by trying new things and expressing gratitude are ways to improve resiliency. Creating a strong bond with your child and providing a caring and supportive relationship while encouraging your child to express opinions and feelings, especially fears, encourages and supports your child learning about resiliency. Secure children are more resilient so routines like a set bedtime for younger children, a list of chores and you being on time and keeping your word are beneficial in building resilience. Reinforce to your child that he is not controlled by his past experience but by his hopes for the future.

How can you tell when your child's resilience reserves are depleted? If you see a number of these signs, you need to help your child build up her reserves again.

- Sleep problems or nightmares

- Change in appetite
- Crying easily over small things
- Becoming easily startled and overly alert
- Can't make decisions or unable to focus
- Anger, resentment and irritability
- Low energy, withdrawn
- Recurring thoughts of failure
- Feeling depressed or anxious

If you see these signs, rev up your exercises to help your child extinguish his pessimistic view of the world using the tools listed above.

Family resilience is also important. Children learn from you and as parent, you must model resilience when you are faced with challenges and setbacks. Children sense your fears and this in turn makes them feel less secure. Talking about your fears during the family meeting can be helpful for the entire family. Talking about your struggles at the dinner table or at random times is not very helpful to the family.

For example, you have been out of work for 8 months and the bank is foreclosing on your home. Since you lost your job you have given brief weekly updates about your job search at the weekly family meetings such as "I found 3 good leads this week" or "no good job prospects this week but there are new openings every week so I'll keep looking" or "the job interview went well, now we just have to wait and see if I'm offered the position." Providing this brief announcement at the same time each week leads to a more secure household that will be able to bounce back better when you have to announce that the family will be moving to a new home. Conversely, random conversations about your job search, even with reassurance that things will work out, still generate a lot of constant worry for the family. Announcing to your children that you are now being foreclosed on could have a devastating effect on the family because they are not prepared for the consequence that 8 months of unemployment and uncertainty about the future has now led them to lose their home.

What you think is how you feel and behave – the ABCs

Flourishing families do a lot of problem solving together. Family problem solving increases engagement. It builds self-esteem and well-being which leads to more positive emotional experiences. Flourishing families provide a lot of emotional support to each other. This emotional support leads to deeper levels of self-determination, self-awareness and independence for each family member. Working within a common framework via an understanding of a cognitive behavioral therapy (CBT) technique called cognitive restructuring can simplify knowing how to explore a problem to provide a quality level of support.

CBT is a strategy that combines behavioral therapy, introduced by Dr. Edward Thorndike and cognitive therapy, introduced by Dr. Albert Ellis and Dr. Aaron Beck. Multiple clinical trials have shown that CBT alone is about equally as effective as medication alone in the treatment of depression and anxiety. CBT helps people look at their thoughts about a situation and determine if those thoughts are rational or irrational. Then it helps people replace irrational thoughts with more rational thoughts. The goal is to change one's thinking to change one's life. The simple formula follows.

Your child loves science and has always been a "straight A" science student. Lately you notice he seems to have lost interest in science and is doing his science homework last instead of first. You ask why his interest has waned.

Adverse event: Your child got a C on a science exam.

Belief: Your child thinks to himself, "I didn't get an A so I am failing."

Consequence: Your child stops studying science as enthusiastically.

So how do you get your child motivated to study hard at science again?

Dispute: His irrational thought that a C on a test means he is failing and replace it with more rational thinking (one C does not a failure make).

Effect: Your child starts doing science homework first again.

An additional technique used in CBT you can apply in your family is called exposure therapy. Exposure therapy is a brief, highly effective strategy used to treat phobias and other anxiety disorders. Through a succession of presentations to a feared object or situation without any danger, conquering a fear occurs. To use exposure therapy, you set up a hierarchy of exposure and work each step of the hierarchy. Your child maintains complete control of when to go to the next step.

Explain to your child that she is to determine on a scale of 1 to 10 how anxious or scared she is when you ask her to participate in each level of the hierarchy. Repeat the item on the hierarchy until her fear is reduced to one. Then ask her if she is ready to go to the next item on the hierarchy. If she says no, use the ABC technique and help her identify the thoughts that are preventing her from going to the next level. Don't spend more than 10 minutes a day on the hierarchy and don't do it more than once a day. You may go through several items in the hierarchy in a single session. If she can't seem to get to a 1 on an item on the hierarchy list, drop down to the previous item and then move back up when she agrees to try it again. Two scenarios follow to demonstrate how exposure therapy can be used to conquer phobias and irrational fears. You may choose to seek out professional assistance to complete this intervention.

Your child has an irrational fear of rabbits and panics every time she sees one. Recently she was given a stuffed rabbit as a gift and she became highly anxious when she opened the box and saw the stuffed toy.

Exposure plan

Step One

- Put the toy away (but not in her room) for now but don't discard it
- Using the ABC technique, determine what your child's beliefs are
- Help her dispute her irrational beliefs
- Ask her if she wants to see the stuffed rabbit
- If yes, allow her to open the box
- If no, or if she exhibits discomfort, put the toy up again and go to Step Two

Step Two

- Develop and implement an exposure hierarchy

Exposure therapy works better if the person receiving the intervention keeps her eyes closed throughout the entire session. Your child is asked to report when she is at 1 on the 1-10 point scale (10=highly anxious and 1= relaxed). This gives your child an opportunity to experience relaxation and know what a 1 feels like to her. Your child is guided into a relaxed state by focusing on breathing deeply about ten times (or until she says the word "one".) She is instructed to "close your eyes and relax." She is asked to remember a pleasant experience, like a recent visit to a park or an ice cream cone she really enjoyed. Repeat "breathe out all your fears and worries" each time she exhales and "breathe in relaxation and calming feelings" each time she inhales. In this example, an exposure hierarchy might include

1. Read her a short story that includes but does not feature a rabbit character.
2. Read her a short story that includes a rabbit as a featured character.
3. Have her imagine a stuffed rabbit on the top shelf of a store she likes to shop in.
4. Have her imagine that a stuffed rabbit is in a box in the parents' room.
5. Have her imagine the stuffed rabbit is on the parents' bed and out of the box.
6. Have her imagine the stuffed rabbit is in a box on her closet shelf.

7. Have her imagine the stuffed rabbit is out of the box on the closet shelf.

8. Have her imagine the stuffed rabbit is in the box and on her bed.

9. Have her imagine the stuffed rabbit is out of the box and on her bed.

10. Have her imagine the stuffed rabbit is in the box on her bed and she is looking into her room.

11. Have her imagine the stuffed rabbit is out of the box on her bed and she is looking into her room.

12. Have her imagine the stuffed rabbit is out of the box on her bed and she is sitting on the bed.

13. Have her imagine the stuffed rabbit is out of the box on her bed and she reaches over to touch the stuffed rabbit.

14. Have her imagine she is sitting on her bed and picks up the stuffed rabbit and begins playing with it.

If you want to help her extinguish her live rabbit phobia once and for all, the next steps to the hierarchy could be added.

15. Have her imagine going to a petting zoo or pet store and petting some animals she likes (this will probably elicit a 1).

16. Have her imagine going to a petting zoo or pet store and looking at the rabbits from a distance.

17. Have her imagine going to a petting zoo or pet store and standing next to the rabbits.

18. Have her imagine going to a petting zoo or pet store and touching a rabbit.

19. Take her to a petting zoo or pet store and ask her if she wants to look at rabbits.

20. Take her to a petting zoo or pet store and ask her if she wants to pet a rabbit.

Your child was born to be an actor. Even as a young child he would demonstrate his talent. He entertains the extended family at every gathering. He puts on plays in the backyard to amuse his friends. He has been invited to join the Drama Club and you enthusiastically agree. The Drama Club is planning the first play of the season. Your child informs you that he is going to work backstage, helping build the set. You ask why he did not try out for a part in the play and discover that he has a fear of public speaking and becomes nervous when thinking about having to stand in front of an audience of strangers. Using the two-step process described above, this is what the hierarchy might look like.

1. Imagine yourself in a small auditorium where all your friends and family are gathered and you walk into the back of the auditorium.

2. Imagine yourself in a small auditorium where all your friends and family are gathered and you walk to the front of the auditorium.

3. Imagine yourself in a small auditorium where all your friends and family are gathered and you turn around to see which friends and family are here.

4. Imagine yourself in a small auditorium where all your friends and family are gathered and you

walk up the steps and onto the stage but your back is to the audience.

5. Imagine yourself in a small auditorium where all your friends and family are gathered and you walk to the stage curtains and go behind the curtains without turning around to see who is in the audience.

6. Imagine yourself in a small auditorium where all your friends and family are gathered and you walk from behind the curtains and down the steps into the audience.

7. Imagine yourself in a small auditorium where all your friends and family are gathered and you walk back up the steps and across the stage to the other side.

8. Imagine yourself in a small auditorium where all your friends and family are gathered and you walk back to the center of the stage, look at your family and friends and say "Hi friends and family, I'm glad you could make it" and then walk off the stage and down the steps.

9. Imagine yourself in a small auditorium where all your friends and family are gathered and each

one of your family and friends have brought one guest. Go up the stairs and onto the stage. Turn around and say "Hi friends, family and guests, I'm glad you could make it" and exit the stage through the stage curtain.

10. Imagine yourself in an auditorium where all your friends and family are gathered with their guests and that your family and friends have each brought three guests. Walk onto the stage from behind the curtain and say "Hi, I'm glad you all could make it" and exit through the stage curtain.

11. Imagine yourself in an auditorium where all your friends and family and their guests are gathered and you walk back on stage and read a short passage from a play and then exit through the stage curtains.

12. Imagine yourself in an auditorium where all your friends, family and guests are gathered and you walk from behind the curtain and cite a short passage you have memorized and then exit through the stage curtains.

13. Imagine yourself in a small auditorium where all your friends, family and guests are gathered and

you walk out on stage to cite your short scene again but this time when you come out from behind the curtain you recite your scene to a full auditorium.

Developing an exposure hierarchy is not a difficult process and I often see complete remission of a phobia after two or three sessions that last less than 30 minutes with adults. As children have less capacity to sit still and focus for 30 minutes, you may want to stick to the ten minute timeframe mentioned above. Having worked with hundreds of people to help them overcome phobias, I have never seen this technique fail.

Note: If the exposure therapy procedure is not crystal clear to you, you are afraid you will do something wrong and make matters worse or you just are not comfortable doing this with your child, don't. Instead seek out a family therapist or family coach trained in cognitive behavioral therapy and skilled at constructing exposure hierarchies.

WARNING: Exposure therapy is different from Flooding Therapy. Flooding is a technique where you expose a person to the feared object or situation head on, without all the small steps in between. Flooding does not use the relaxation technique or allow the individual to be in control of the situation.

Your child is afraid to swim. Exposure therapy allows your child to imagine swimming while in a relaxed state and safe environment before the child is taken to a pool to watch friends having fun in the water. Exposure lets her gradually get used to being in the water, one foot at a time and only when she is ready. Flooding would involve taking your child to the pool, planting an accomplice in the deep end for safety's sake and pushing your child into the deep end of the pool, instructing her to "sink or swim." Flooding can be highly traumatic.

Learn to avoid automatic thinking

Automatic thinking is thinking that is not challenged and underlies our level of conscious awareness. Automatic thoughts are unintentional, effortless and involuntary. These cognitive distortions cause unhappiness and lower our sense of self. Automatic thinking stifles resiliency. Our sense of well-being is diminished when negative insidious thoughts take control. Automatic negative thinking leads to anxiety and depression. Types of automatic negative thinking (ANTs) include:

Overgeneralization – Coming to a generalized conclusion based on a single event. Your child is turned down for a date and thinks "I'll always be lonely"

Magnification – Exaggerating the importance of negative experiences while minimizing the importance of positive experience. In past years your child has made a C in English but this year is making higher marks and thinks "What's wrong, I'm not good at English. I'm sure I'll start getting a C again"

Catastrophe thinking – Overestimating an outcome. Your child has his first pimple and it is barely noticeable. Today he is getting a class picture made for the yearbook. He thinks "I'll be the laughing stock of the school for years to come."

All or nothing thinking – Something is black or white and there is no middle ground. Your child has stopped playing with a friend and you ask why. Your child tells you her friend told her she had big feet. Your child thinks "She's not my friend anymore."

Mindreading – Presuming you know what the other is thinking without asking what the other is thinking. Your child has a crush on someone at school and sees him sitting with another classmate on a bench in the mall. Your child thinks "He likes her more than me."

"I should have or be" – Focusing on how things should be rather than acknowledging how they actually are. Your child won second place in the spelling bee thinks "I should have won because I got a hard word and my competitor got an easy word. Life isn't fair."

"I can't stand it" – Believing you don't have the capacity to tolerate something. Your child doesn't like the smell of cabbage and won't sit near it when cabbage is on the dinner table. Your child thinks "I can't stand the smell of cabbage and it shouldn't be served except when I am not home."

Not paying attention to our ANTs fuels automatic thinking. Automatic thinking charges negative emotion and contributes to depression and anxiety. Acknowledging to ourselves that our first (automatic) thought may not be correct and looking at alternative explanations destroys automatic thinking. The first step to overcoming automatic thinking is to pay attention to the underlying thoughts that contribute to negative emotional experience by using the ABC technique described above. Help your child identify automatic negative thinking and construct alternative beliefs. You might playfully point out to her when the ANTs are crawling around in your child's mind. If you don't, your child may experience something called learned helplessness.

Extinguish learned helplessness and replace it with mastery

Helplessness is not a personality trait but a belief that is nurtured. While automatic thoughts are triggered by some action in the world, learned helplessness is a pervasive response that is determined at some point as truth, without questioning the helplessness again. Once we have learned to be helpless over a situation, activity or feeling, behaviors follow to prove the belief is correct and we experience negative feelings when confronted with that situation, activity or feeling. Once helplessness sets in, we are not even aware that it is the driver for us to not accomplish something we think we want or need to do. We believe that nothing we do will matter so we do nothing.

Your child throws and catches baseballs with you in the backyard and seems to enjoy the activity. He doesn't seem to really care that he is not particularly good at it. You encourage him that the more practice he has the better he will get at throwing and catching the baseball. When you suggest that he try out for a sport team at school he replies that he is not good at sports and doesn't want to try out. You nudge him to try out nonetheless. He does and comes home to tell you "there, I didn't get on the team. I told you I was lousy at sports and I don't ever want to try out again."

Using the ABC technique, you learn that your child does not enjoy sports where he has to be a member of a team. Having identified this thought, you can reverse his learned helpless thought "I'm lousy at sports so I won't try again" and correct it with "maybe I haven't found a sport where my individual contribution would make sports more fun for me."

Just as we learn to be helpless, we can unlearn to be helpless once we identity where the helplessness stems from. Helplessness is not based on a fear of failure but on our view of how things work in the world. We approach our world either through helplessness or mastery. We may be masterful in some areas of our lives and feel helpless in others. Three ideas of how we view the world develop helplessness or mastery.

Stability is whether we believe an outcome is temporary or permanent. Pessimists tend to see a negative outcome as permanent, and become helpless while optimists see a negative outcome as temporary and an opportunity to try something different. Conversely, pessimists see a positive outcome as temporary and optimists see a positive outcome as having a permanent effect on well-being.

Globality is our view of what kind of effect an outcome has on our overall life satisfaction and well-being. Optimists believe that every outcome is a separate event and that negative outcomes are specific to a situation and have a small but cumulative effect on well-being and life satisfaction. Pessimists believe that outcomes are more global and that a negative outcome has a wide effect on life satisfaction and well-being, thus developing helplessness.

Locus of control is whether you believe that an outcome is attributed to internal or external factors. Optimists think that positive outcomes happen because of what they did (I made it happen) while pessimists think that positive outcomes are due to external influences (I'm lucky) and this contributes to a sense of helplessness.

Some thoughts that lead to becoming helpless include

- I have little control over the things that happen to me.
- There is really no way I can solve some of the problems I have.

- There is little I can do to change many of the important things in my life.
- I often feel helpless in dealing with the problems of life.
- Sometimes I feel that I am being pushed around in life.

Thoughts that inoculate us from becoming helpless include

- What happens to me in the future mostly depends on me.
- I can do just about anything I really set my mind to do.
- I expect much from life.
- I am full of plans for my future.
- I often feel that life is full of promise.
- I can make this happen

Children experiencing helplessness have poor problem solving skills, less school satisfaction, few friends, and diminished interpersonal skills. Studies show that persons experiencing helplessness have weakened immune systems leading to more infections and colds with longer recovery periods from health problems. Adults who are helpless experience more heart problems and die younger than those who do not experience helplessness.

Moreover, helpless children don't act on their desires, believing nothing they do will matter. They are shy, withdrawn, passive and disengaged. Children who experience helplessness have a much higher incidence of failing at school and teens have a much higher dropout rate if they are experiencing helplessness. Helplessness threatens well-being and results in feelings of worthlessness. This leads to depression or anxiety and ultimately to hopelessness.

The following characteristics are found in children who are experiencing helplessness

- Low self-esteem
- Low motivation to learn
- Test anxiety
- Passivity

- Depression or anxiety

- Lack of confidence

- Low expectations

- Low resilience

- A focus on what they can't do

- Self-blame, even when it is not their fault

From the first day you interact with your child you are setting the stage for them to learn about mastery and helplessness. When children observe that they have little control over their environment, they become helpless.

You have a fussy baby that cries through the night. No matter how you console him, he cries almost every hour. You ask everyone you know how to stop the crying and nothing they suggest works either. You give up trying and let your child cry through the night, feeling guilty and helpless. You may even begin to doubt your abilities as a parent.

Your baby has another viewpoint. He learned that when he cried, you came into the room and held him, talked to him and interacted with him. He had mastery over getting your attention. Eventually he stops crying because he has learned that he no longer gets the desired result from you. Crying is a helpless activity for him because he can't use crying to let you know that he is hungry, angry, bored or scared when he awakens in the night.

Your job is to set up experiences for your child that helps him cultivate mastery and defeat helplessness when it germinates. Mastery is about feeling in control, within the limitations the parents have set for their children. Mastery is self-taught but you can help out. For younger children use toys that are interactive and that allow a child to produce an action to get a response from the toy. The child controls the outcome, getting the toy to produce the desired outcome. Computers and computer games are great for older children to experience choice and learn about the consequences of their choices.

To reinforce mastery, allow children to fail and don't fix the problem for them. Talk with them about the problem and help them identify other ways to approach the problem but don't do the work for them. Children need to become uncomfortable with a situation before they are willing to change it. Let them become just uncomfortable enough that they initiate a problem solving process. While mastery predicts a probability of a different outcome when a specific action takes place, helplessness predicts that the outcome will be the same whether a response is made or not, since the desired outcome has not been achieved by past actions.

Fixing any problem and achieving any goal will have setbacks or sub-failures. Help your child break down the outcome into small achievable goals so that when a sub-failure occurs, she will have evidence to demonstrate she is on the right path. This builds not only mastery but resilience as well and she will bounce back from a sub-failure more quickly.

To develop mastery in your child, maximize the amount of choice your child has and tolerate when a response is no. If you expect your child to do something, direct them instead of requesting something from them. When you ask questions like "Don't you want to ____" or "Why don't we _____" you must respect when they say no. When you are preparing a family meal at home and you have several vegetables to choose from, ask which one your child wants instead of making the decision for the whole family. Sometimes choices are limited to two possibilities. Your child breaks a family rule and knows the consequence. It is your child's choice to accept the consequence or follow the rule. Even if he has a very good reason for breaking a family rule, he still made the choice that accepting a consequence was more important than following the family rule. Choices always exist.

For mastery to occur you need to allow for exploration, even if it is worrisome to you. Children need to be able to explore new ideas, behaviors and environments. Encourage exploration and your child will feel more in control of her life. Exploration should not violate family norms or rules and as the parent you determine how far the exploration goes. From the crib to the playpen, from the playpen to the living room floor, from the living room floor to the park, from the park to school, from school to dating, from dating to moving away from home all represent your ability to let your child explore and gain mastery over her life.

As a parent focusing on helping your child gain mastery, you may find some delightful changes in your own mastery. The tools you teach your child can be equally valuable in helping you let go of areas where you feel helpless or immobilized and make you a much better model for how your children can flourish as adults.

Practice calming and focusing strategies

Ruminating thoughts, anxiety, hopelessness and helplessness diminish our capacity to remain resilient and wear down our reserves. Encourage your child to routinely practice calming techniques such as meditation or prayer, walking, mindfulness, relaxation techniques, tai chi or yoga. Families that participate in similar calming and focusing activities get the best benefit.

Mindfulness is an intentional procedure that helps increase baseline clarity and experience better tolerance of moment to moment outcomes. In psychology, mindfulness is used as a treatment strategy for people diagnosed with anxiety, obsessive compulsive disorders, depression, post-traumatic stress, substance use disorders and for people struggling with troubling personality disorder characteristics. You can practice formal mindfulness meditation at the same time every day. You can also incorporate mindfulness throughout the day in some very simple ways.

Formal mindfulness meditation procedure

- Find a quiet spot where you will not be disturbed for at least ten minutes.

- Focus on your breath and acknowledge your inhalation and exhalation. You can say to yourself "in" on the inhale and "out" on the exhale.

- Begin to notice the thoughts, feelings and attitudes that come into your mind. Just observe the thoughts, without judgment.

- Become aware that thoughts are not facts and thoughts are not permanent

- You may choose to categorize your thoughts and name them such as "this is a thought about work", "this is a thought about dinner", "this is a thought about my sadness"

Impromptu mindfulness techniques include

- Eat mindfully. Observe every morsel on your plate and eat each bite with all your senses including smell, taste, mouth feel, visual appeal and feelings associated with eating the food.

- Walk mindfully. Become fully aware of your foot on the ground, the experience of lifting a foot off the ground, how your leg muscles respond, how your arms respond, how your breath responds to your walking. Take in all the sights, smells, sounds and visual experiences without looking into the distance. Be totally focused on just where you are, at this moment.

- Take a breathing break for one minute. During this minute, focus on your breath and nothing else.

Mindfulness helps turn a worried mind into a clear mind and has lasting effects that gradually increase throughout the day the longer you practice it. You can expect to experience a calm awareness of your body, thoughts, feelings, attitudes and behaviors.

Teach Self Determination

Self-determination is the right for us to direct our own lives. It is the ability to identify and achieve goals based on a foundation of knowing and valuing ourselves. Teaching your children self-determination helps them become empowered. They become aware of their strengths and challenges and act on their decisions. When a child is encouraged to exhibit attitudes and abilities that allow her to become the causal agent in her life, without undue influence or interference, she is able to build mastery. Components of self-determination on your child's part include

- Choice making
- Problem solving
- Decision making
- Goal setting

- Self advocacy

- Self control

- Self awareness

- Self knowledge

As your child learns about self-determination she has the opportunity to know herself better, value herself and her place in the family, plan under her own initiative, act on those plans and evaluate the outcomes of her action. A very young child might experience self-determination through self calming while an older child might learn about self-determination by being allowed to plan out some of the family activities of the week.

Teens in families that embrace the concept of self-determination have less problems individuating from the family. Individuation is a process that children go through when they realize that while they are still a part of the family, they are also autonomous from the family. Individuation can be a grueling process for both parent and child in that the child may be confused and uncertain about taking on the responsibility of determining her future and parents have a hard time of letting go of making decisions for their child. Studies show that children who are taught self-determination skills have a better chance of succeeding as they transition into adulthood.

Self-determination is a two way street for families. Parents who fail to provide adequate support to practice ever increasing amounts of self- determination promoting activities sabotage even the most skillful of children who are self-determined. Your child needs to be allowed to integrate the experience of self-determination into his self-concept to understand the sub-concepts of free will, freedom of choice, independence and individual responsibility.

The experience of self-determination can only be had when reasonable risks are taken, mistakes are made and learning from the outcomes takes place. The self-determination matrix includes setting goals, making decisions about which goals to reach for, looking at options to achieve the goal, solving problems around the barriers to reaching the selected goal, understanding the supports needed from others to accomplish those goals, being assertive when others try to take charge of the outcome and evaluating the outcomes as a result of an action. Parents are only responsible for providing opportunities for their children to practice self-determination and to provide a safety net if things get too far off track.

There are other tasks for parents when teaching self-determination. Promote choice in the household by helping your child identify her strengths, talents and abilities, by offering opportunities for a child to make choices (such as clothing, social activities, participating in some family events, friendships) and by allowing for mistakes with natural consequence. Explore the possibilities of life with your child by talking about future possible occupations, hobbies your child may be interested in, clubs that support her interest. Encourage problem solving by helping your child accept that problems are a healthy part of life and help us grow while allowing your child to take ownership of the challenges and problems she faces. Expand self advocacy skills by pointing out instances where your child has demonstrated assertiveness and providing leadership opportunities for some family activities.

Self-determination of the individual may seem incompatible with harmonious dependence on the family and incongruent with internalizing self-determination within the family. However, self-determination is not willfulness but a willingness to take responsibility and to take risks. Teaching your child to be self-determined is one of the most important lessons your child will learn.

Increase family vitality

Family vitality is essential to the flourishing family. The vitality of the family directly supports each family member's desire to be a part of it. A family with low vitality isn't much fun to be in and parents who maintain a low vitality household often wonder why their children do not want to spend much time at home. Unlike ideal families portrayed on television, where everyone lives in harmony, a conflict arises and is resolved in a few moments and every one resumes family harmony by the end of the show, real families struggle with vitality. Family researchers refer to high vitality families as strong families and have determined a number of characteristics that strong families share in common.

Whether you are a single parent, living in a two parent household, each parent is living in a different household or you are maintaining a blended family, you can still develop family vitality. Strong family environments create a sense of togetherness and belonging for all the family members. It helps the family problem solve efficiently and adapt to changes as the members of the family change. The following is a generally recognized list of characteristics strong families share in common.

- Commitment to the family
- Expressed appreciation of what others in the family do for you
- A desire to spend time together as a family
- Good communication
- A healthy lifestyle

- Strong similar values and spiritual understanding
- An optimistic outlook
- Celebration and acceptance of each person's unique strengths
- Involvement with friends and community
- Ability to forgive others in the family
- Having fun together

Additionally, in a two parent household where people live together there needs to be a strong relationship between the adult partners as evidenced by clear communication between the adults, mutual expressed respect for each other and self-disclosure of thoughts and feelings between the couple. In cases of divorced parents, strong families demonstrate a cooperative relationship and an ability to put the needs of the children above the hurt feelings of the parents.

For a family to retain high vitality, they spend quality time together doing things such as walking or exercising together, reading together, preparing meals together, attending activities together and visiting friends and relatives together. To demonstrate commitment they solve family problems together and parents encourage exploration and curiosity. Parents remind children they are there for them and make time to listen when the child needs support. Parents encourage children to be a part of their own spiritual practices whether it's affiliating with a religious institution or being renewed by a weekend hike in the forest.

Expressed communication, not just what you say but how you say it, increases or decreases family vitality. Using active listening skills with each other such as not interrupting while a family member is talking, listening for both verbal statements and non-verbal cues and paraphrasing what you heard the other say to be certain you understood the point raises vitality in the family. Family members who know that what they have to say is valued by the other family members, leads to a desire to communicate more within the family. The use of "I" statements over "You" statements reinforce family commitment and connection. Asking questions like "How was school today?" may elicit one word responses like "good" or "ok" but that same question when rephrased to "Tell me about what happened in school today" requires a broader response and vitalizes your relationship.

Strong families don't hesitate to express appreciation to each other. They are not afraid to tell each other they love them. Strong families say thank you to each other frequently and spontaneously. Parents thank children when they complete a chore, even if it is on the chore list in the Family Charter. Children thank each other and the parent when complimented, allowed a privilege or have been extended an act of kindness. They may do this verbally, via a thank you note if the other is not around to be thanked or through the expression of a random act of kindness to the giver.

High vitality families know what the word resilience means and practice building it together. They see crisis or disappointment as an opportunity for growth and problem solving. They offer each other solace and encouragement when a family member experiences an adverse outcome. They acknowledge and celebrate victories of other family members. They talk about the lessons learned from a setback.

Extend Positive Relationships

Good relationships within the family leads to social competence, cooperation and helpfulness. Children who are not well bonded to the family seek out peers who are also alienated or disenfranchised. But positive relationship extends far beyond the nuclear family.

Research finds that 10% of children in the United States have no friends in school, 75% of all children in the US experience some form of harassment before they become adults and 30% of US children below the age of sixteen reports having been bullied. As a parent you, or a trusted care giver, controls most of the experience your very young child has. That control ends when you child starts school. Less time is spent with you and more time is spent with classmates and teachers. By adolescence, 30% of time is spent with peers.

Studies show that children who have positive relationships with their parents experience more positive mental health, better physical health, higher educational outcomes and deeper religious or spiritual convictions. These children also have less substance abuse and a more responsible approach to sex in adolescence and early adulthood.

In two parent families where children do not have positive relationships with both parents or where there is marital discord, children have worse outcomes related to mental and physical health, educational outcomes and an overall lower sense of well-being. Extending positive relationships begins in the home and spills over into all aspects of your child's environment.

Children are intuitive and pick up on the two parent relationship. It is difficult to extend positive relationships to your children if you don't have a positive relationship with your adult partner living in your home. Children believe that their two parents have relationship harmony when they agree on certain relational attributes including how they

- Handle family finances

- Share common interest in recreational activities

- Agree on religious or spiritual matters

- Demonstrate affection

- Have common friends

- Agree on how they view correct or proper behavior

- Define a common philosophy of life

- Deal with parents and in-laws in a similar manner

- Place importance on spending time together

- Make major decisions together

- Refuse to leave home after a fight

- Confide in each other

- Show they trust each other

- Exhibit commitment to making the relationship last

Beyond the internal structure of the family as an extension of positive relationship building, the second most important vehicle for your child is typically the school they attend. Be involved with the school your child attends. Build a positive relationship with your children's teachers and create a healthy home-school connection. If you feel unvalued or unwelcome at your child's school create a change, even if it means talking about your experience and perception to the principal or guidance counselor. You may have had negative experiences with school yourself or have a negative view of teachers and the school system. Examine your own prejudices, if you have any, and realize you are not bound by your past experience as an indicator of your child's experience at school. Working with your child's teacher requires reciprocal respect, cooperation, shared responsibility for your child's education and negotiation of conflict between your child's teacher and you.

Expanding positive relationships are often easily found when including non-toxic members of your extended family. Extended families may include grandparents, aunts and uncles, cousins and godparents but many families form strong positive relationships with other families and neighbors. Build more positive relationships by identifying families who share common interests with you. Children benefit from observing multiple adult role models and parents benefit from having adult time with other adults who share similar interests.

Generate more positive emotions in your family

Building positive emotional experience naturally occurs when you use all of the above techniques. Nonetheless, you will want to set the stage for your child to recognize, acknowledge and appreciate positive emotional experience more mindfully. Positive emotional experience comes in many forms. You may see your child become ecstatic when he accomplishes something he thought would be very difficult or even impossible. You child may be moved to overwhelming joy when visiting a theme park for the first time. These peak positive emotional experiences, unfortunately, are short lived and rarely experienced. If your child only associates positive emotions with peak experiences, he will soon fall into a pessimistic world view. However, just reliving a peak experience has been shown to increase positive emotion.

Take positive emotions as seriously as you take your child's negative emotions. Acknowledge your child's positive emotions and use Dr. Barbara Fredrickson's Broaden and Build model which is demonstrated to create more well-being and life satisfaction. Simply put, the broaden and build model says that the experience of positive emotion leads people to broaden their thinking and actions. These thoughts and actions help them build strengths and acquire resources.

Positive emotions broaden awareness and encourage new, different and exploratory thought and actions. Over time this builds skills and resources. For example, you meet a stranger at the park and have a pleasant conversation that leads to a positive emotional experience. The next time you see this person in the park, you have another positive emotional experience. This continues for some time and you and your new friend begin doing other things together as well. The positive emotional experience prompted you to repeat the experience and over time you acquired a resource, your new friend.

While the effects of positive emotion is typically not apparent until long after the experience of the positive emotion itself, negative emotions have an immediate effect on our environment and how we respond to it. Fear is primal. When we experience fear, we have a tendency to respond with a specific action. Whether we fight or flee is based on a number of external as well as internal factors. If a bee hovers around you and you are afraid you'll get stung, your tendency is to fight off the bee. If a bear starts following you on a hike, you are more likely to flee than to fight. It is the almost instinctual flight or fight response that keeps us alive when we are in danger. Negative emotions, like anger and sadness, are "need to act now" driven and narrow our responses to the driver of the feeling. When we experience anger it is a message that we are being attacked or trespassed against. We protect, withdraw, attack back or respond assertively.

One study on broadening and building positive emotional experiences placed volunteers into one of three groups. One group did nothing (this is called the control group). The second group was told to write down a list of hassles they experienced each day. The third group was instructed to write down a "count your blessings" list each day. The groups were followed and those in the "count your blessings" group reported fewer physiological and psychological complaints and better sleep. The differences in the outcomes for this group over the other two groups was not the result of the power of positive thinking but the power of expressing gratitude and the resultant positive emotional experience associated with that behavior.

Findings from other studies prove that people who practice cultivating positive emotional experience

- Live longer
- Experience thought that is flexible, creative, efficient
- Are more resilient
- Have better attention and focus
- Increase their scope of cognition and interconnectedness

- Experience better relationships

Dr. Abraham Maslow's hierarchy of needs include survival, safety, belonging, self-esteem and self-actualizing. The lowest and most basic needs are often met though the experience of negative emotions, driven by fear and anger. As these needs are predictably met, we begin to focus on the upper three levels on the hierarchy and these are typically accomplished as a result of positive emotional experience.

How do you fill you and your child's world with positive emotional experience? Relaxation exercises lead to contentment. Finding positive meaning to an adverse event leads to positive emotion. There is evidence that a simple genuine smile releases chemicals in the brain that are associated with positive emotional experience. Doing something you love to do each day produces positive emotions. Frequent expressions of gratitude render positive emotion. Being in the moment and lingering there a few additional seconds, pumps up positive emotion. Doing things that allow you to use your core strengths is invaluable to producing positive emotion. Asking yourself each day if you are moving toward happiness or negativity, and correcting negative behaviors that result in negative feelings builds positive emotions.

The components of an emotional state include feeling, sensory, thinking and action. Negative emotions are intolerant and have narrow attention while positive emotions are expansive, tolerant and interactive. Positive emotions lead to better health, higher productivity, better coping skills during times of adversity and improved social resources. Focusing on positive emotions eliminates thoughts about hostility, ill will, anger and resentment.

A sure fire technique for expanding positive emotion experience is practicing daily Loving Kindness Meditation also known as Metta Bhavana. You don't have to get on the floor and fold your legs in a full lotus position for this to work. You don't have to wear a saffron robe or convert to Buddhism. It's simple, and you will get better at it each day you practice loving kindness meditation. I use it twice a day, when I arise and before I fall asleep at night. I might also bestow it on myself and another individual in the middle of the day, like when I'm in a hurry and someone in front of me at the checkout counter of the supermarket pulls out 40 coupons to redeem.

Loving Kindness meditation is brief. You simply recite specific words to cultivate compassion and increase positive emotional experience. It has been demonstrated scientifically that using this technique stimulates the parts of the brain associated with compassion and empathy that the brain can be permanently changed through this practice and that compassion can be learned.

People who add this technique to their daily routine can expect to become more mindful, have better self-acceptance, more positive relationships, more positive health outcomes and higher life satisfaction. To complete a loving kindness meditation, follow these steps.

How to Complete a Loving Kindness Meditation

Find a quiet time and place where you will be uninterrupted for at least ten minutes. Get comfortable. I like to complete about 10 deep breathing exercises before I begin the meditation, telling myself to breathe in relaxation on each inhalation and breathe out distractions and stress on each exhalation.

I recite three statements about what I want for myself:

1. May I be free from inner and outer harm
2. May I be healthy and strong, mentally and physically
3. May I be able to take care of myself, joyfully

I then repeat this recitation thinking about someone I highly regard (different people at different times). Sometimes when I am not feeling good about myself or my life situation, I reverse the process and begin with the person I highly regard and then say it about myself as the second recitation.

I then recite the same three wishes while thinking about someone I dearly love, followed by a neutral person or acquaintance I know.

The next recitation is about someone I am angry with (like the coupon queen mentioned above) or someone I am working on forgiving.

The final recitation is aimed toward everyone and everything in the universe (even the bugs that are eating my plants). Essentially, you are generalizing to all sentient beings that you wish them freedom from harm, suffering, disease and pain and hoping that they experience happiness, joy, serenity and prosperity.

Forgive others and don't hold grudges

Forgiveness is a gift you give yourself and failure to forgive always leads to negative emotional experiences. Holding a grudge is self-imposed and releasing a grudge is self-bestowed. Teaching your child how to release himself from a betrayal or failed expectation, the primary reasons someone is the recipient of lack of forgiveness or grudges, is vital to your child's well-being.

Forgiveness isn't about saying the action from the other is acceptable. Instead forgiveness acknowledges that you have learned from the experience, integrated the experience into your life and let go of the negative feelings regarding the incident. Forgiveness doesn't guarantee reconciliation or rebuild trust with the offender. Instead it releases you from negative feeling and puts you back in control; you are no longer a victim. Forgiveness allows you to let go of resentment and thoughts of revenge. Refusing to forgive eats at your well-being, robs you of peacefulness and results in negative emotional experience including anger, sadness, confusion and immobility. Refusal to forgive brings your hurt and resentment into new relationships and you become less trusting of others. People who practice forgiveness find that they have healthier relationships, better psychological well-being, less anxiety, stress, hostility, fear, lowered health risks and less substance abuse.

Challenges to forgiveness are many. People fear that forgiveness equates to acceptance, that the offending person is "off the hook" and allows the offender to not admit they were wrongful in their actions. People are less likely to forgive if there is no just compensation, either begging forgiveness or guaranteeing different behavior in the future. People are less likely to be able to forgive if the offender exhibits lack of remorse on their wrongful action.

A formula exists to teach you and your child how to forgive and is ascribed to an acronym called REACH. Reach allows one to forgive and to act with hope for better outcomes and hope for the future.

> Recall the experience objectively, without the emotional charge.
>
> Empathize as if you were the other and understood the motivations for their action.
>
> Altruistic response – a gift when someone forgave you in the past for a transgression and you can forgive the transgressor now.
>
> Commit to tell others you forgave the transgression, even if you don't tell the transgressor.
>
> Hold on to the forgiveness, remembering you have forgiven the transgressor every time a negative feeling about the transgression arises into conscious thought.

> Your 15 year old has just had his heart broken for the first time. An older student worked hard to get your child's girlfriend away from him and she now decides she likes the other teen better than your child. Every day your child sees this boy, he seethes.

He talks to you about how he would like to ambush him and beat him up. He is not sleeping well through the night and he doesn't show much appetite. You point out that he is causing his rage and health problems and that only he has the power to restore balance and move on to find another girl to like. Using the REACH model, he regains his self-control and releases himself from the negative emotions attached to the grudge.

Confront a crisis head-on

Almost all families face crisis or catastrophic events. Common crisis themes are centered on health problems, financial difficulties, relationship discord such as divorce, a child running away, or increased misbehavior unacceptable to the family and accidents such as someone being injured or devastation of property due to natural disasters.

Let's divide family crisis into two categories and look briefly at each of those categories. Developmental crisis occurs in a family when events like getting married, having a new child come into the home, a child starting school, a child leaving home, parents retiring. Even with careful planning, these events and others put the family into crisis. Structural crisis is abrupt, unanticipated and finds the family unprepared and without the coping skills necessary to meet the challenge the crisis brings. Finding out a spouse is cheating, coping with a shameful event caused by a family member, discovering that a family member is having suicidal thoughts, learning that a family member experienced physical or sexual abuse, announcing a divorce to the family, recognizing that someone in the family is abusing drugs, a family member being arrested, the sudden death of a loved one, loss of property due to a fire or flood are some examples of structural crisis.

Whether the crisis is developmental or structural, the result is that the family is forever changed. When a family is confronted by a crisis, each member must determine the meaning the crisis has for the individual as well as the impact on family dynamics. Flourishing families are more resilient to crisis than families that are floundering. A flourishing family is more likely to talk openly about the crisis, its impact on their family, and what they can do to support each other in moving past the crisis. For floundering families, a family crisis may result in the feeling of a lack of family closeness. Family members may fight over who is right. Families often curtail activities that the family has done together like exercising or going on family outings. Criticism and hostility may be exhibited. Family members may experience trouble eating and sleeping. Family members may become withdrawn or hostile and temporarily stop using conflict resolutions techniques that have worked in the past for the family.

The United States Department of Health and Human Services estimates that a family crisis usually lasts no more than six weeks. There are five phases a family goes through when moving beyond a family crisis. First there is the crisis trigger, an event that compels the family to go into crisis mode. The second phase is the interpretation of the crisis by each family member which results in a realization that the crisis event is a threat to the family's well-being. In the third phase, the family becomes disorganized and roles and self-identity change for some family members. This initially leads to maladaptive behaviors but the family reorganizes in phase four by searching for solutions to the crisis. In the final phase, families adopt the new coping strategies discovered and get on with life.

What can you do to help your family move through a crisis? Don't avoid talking about the crisis. Talk openly, honestly and frequently and express hope for the future. In addition to talking as a family about how to resolve the crisis, talk about the feelings related to the crisis. Include discussion about family changes and dynamics as a result of the crisis. A crisis represents a loss to each member of your family and grieving is a part of dealing with loss. Explore with your family what will be missing, how to compensate for the loss, and what can never be reclaimed as a result of this crisis event. Help your family accept the circumstances for what they are, neither minimizing the impact of the crisis on the family nor exaggerating it's long term effect on your family's well-being.

Identify and use a support network outside the family as well. Find persons that do not judge or criticize the family for the results of the crisis. Encourage the family to maintain daily routines and a healthy lifestyle even through the crisis period. Take control of what it is within your power to control. Pay attention to when a family member needs extra support. Most importantly remember that there is a resolution to every crisis and that a crisis dissipates over time although the effect may be far reaching.

Put the outcome in perspective

Remind your child that each outcome you observe when an activity is attempted by your child is set apart and distinct. It is a series of outcomes that leads to mastery or helplessness. By reinforcing this you will discover that an unanticipated outcome is an opportunity to learn what went wrong and how to correct it in the future. Many factors contribute to the outcome you and your children see from the actions you take.

Conclusion validity is the degree to which the conclusions we draw about the relationships to the actions we took to reach an outcome actually caused the outcome. Sometimes our conclusion from a learned experience is unreasonable. Help your children understand that there is not always a causal relationship for a single outcome. Even the most skilled person sometimes fails if the environment is not conducive to success.

Other factors contribute to the likelihood of successful outcomes. These include doing one thing at a time instead of trying to multi-task or complete too many projects at once. Losing focus on the goal, spending a lot of time on unimportant things and being disorganized lessens the likelihood we will reach our desired outcome. Goals that are specific, measureable, and attainable and can be broken down into small steps improve the probability of a desired outcome. If your child is interrupted frequently or asked to add an ever increasing number of activities, he may become resentful and sabotage his activity, even to the point of blaming others for a failure. Outcome expectancies also contribute to the likelihood of success.

Psychologist Neal Miller and anthropologist John Dollard teamed up to look at how we learn and formulated social cognitive theory. This theory states that people learn new behaviors as a result of drivers, cues, responses and rewards. Assist your child in determining what motivates them to learn a new behavior, what they need to see and understand to accomplish a desired outcome, help shape their responses and determine what the reward (desired outcome) is for learning the new behavior. That is to say that if your child is properly motivated, he will learn through clear observations that he can practice to achieve the desired outcome.

Dr. Albert Bandura expanded on the work of Miller and Dollard to create a theory of social learning. Since most things learned by family members occurs in the social context of the family, it is particularly appropriate that we use some of his discoveries when looking at putting outcomes into perspective. Dr. Bandura believes that moral development is the result of social, cognitive and environmental factors and that this development is enhanced when there is a close identification between the observer (your child) and the model (you). Because of this close identification, your child will exhibit moral performance based on his capabilities, knowledge, skills, awareness of the rules and his ability to take idea to action.

A flourishing parent models putting an outcome into perspective in their adult life and a flourishing child learns to view victories and setbacks as part of the bigger picture. Each outcome contributes to overall well-being but no single outcome controls future well-being and family harmony.

Seven mistakes floundering parents make

A positive child/parent relationship is essential to maintain a flourishing family. There are some common traps that floundering parents fall into. Even a flourishing parent, when confronted with a situation he seems helpless to control may resort to these tactics. If you are including these behaviors in your parenting style, take a step back to determine how you can approach this problem with your child using any of the techniques described above. Families only flounder because of lack knowledge and skills, lack of action on the skill set they have learned or lack of desire to change the family structure.

Talking too much such as nagging, pleading or lecturing doesn't typically produce the desired outcome. If they did, there would be need to nag, plead or lecture. In a family where a Family Charter is consistently utilized, there are no nagging, cajoling or threatening conversations. If you are not getting your demand met, your child has clear consequences. You don't need to have further discussion.

Allowing tirades and temper tantrums is a trap that manipulates a parent into giving in. Parents who are firm in their resolve don't experience tantrums. When one occurs, there is a consequence. Flourishing families treat resistance conversations with their child in the same way they would colleagues at a challenging business meeting. They remain calm, examine the evidence, determine where they are negotiable and non-negotiable and end the meeting when there is no hope of resolution or when compromise is reached.

Tears of frustration on the parents' part or statements about how sad your child's behavior or attitude makes you may even occur in flourishing families, but only on rare occasion. While your child may use tantrums to get his way, crying about your child's behavior in front of him to demonstrate your displeasure is a floundering parent's version of the temper tantrum and raging at your child is your form of a tirade. The more frequently you use these tactics, or try to make your child feel guilty, the more floundering your family becomes. When you appear weak and ineffective, your child learns from this and will likely more frequently "push your buttons". A more effective strategy is to withdraw from the child if you are overwhelmed, compose yourself privately and then talk to your child calmly about your displease, your expectations of how things will change in the future and the consequence your child will face if change is not forthcoming.

Terroristic threats or threats of physical abuse may lead to compliance and helplessness but never to mastery. When a floundering parent tells her child she will beat him to within an inch of his life or that "I brought you into this world and I can take you out" she is sending a clear message that she does not love her child enough to help solve the problem. Instead, she is telling him "I am willing to damage you physically or kill you rather than to continue supporting you as we figure out how to fix this problem." Is this what you really mean? Is this single event so important to her that she will potentially murder her child if he fails to act the way she wants him to?

Inconsistency in your expectations leads to confusion and insecurity on your child's part. Allowing her to break rules or get privileges you know she doesn't deserve gives your child permission to become argumentative and unreliable. Be correct in your actions ensuring that the punishment fits the crime, the reward fits the achievement and all your children are treated justly. Be consistent in your actions and expectations and model this for your child.

Arguing about discipline in front of your child is not beneficial to you and your partner or to your child. When parents argue in front of their child about rules, consequences, rewards or chores, what the child mostly hears is "We are not in alignment in our beliefs regarding parenting." The child also hears about variable discipline strategies and can use this information to triangulate the parents, playing one off the other. Further, your child may draw conclusions about who the "good" parent is and who the "bad" parent is. The "bad" parent is usually the one with the harsher discipline or the lower reward. Your child stores this information and uses it to his advantage when he is asking for a privilege, going to the "softer" parent for high risk requests. Parents do have disagreements about disciplining children and should certainly talk about those differences privately with each other and come to compromise. Only then should the child be involved in knowing what the discipline is. Family Charters are a powerful tool for disciple because your child already knows what to expect when he breaks a family rule and it shows that both parents are exactly on the same page when it concerns discipline.

Treating your kids like you own them extinguishes self-determination and mastery and leads your child to become withdrawn, helpless and passive. By demanding much from your child and giving little in return you are failing to model fairness, integrity, generosity and social or emotional intelligence. Flourishing families celebrate each family member's unique contribution to the family, encourage autonomy and reinforce self-determination. The floundering child either can't wait to leave home or has little initiative to explore the world on his own. The flourishing child savors the family experience and knows he is a cherished part of a bigger family system.

Strengths based living

In the previous section of this book, you learned about 18 ways floundering families transform into flourishing families and flourishing families stay on course. This section of the book helps you identify signature character strengths of each family member and how to capitalize on those strengths to build individual and family well-being.

Before you begin reading the rest of this section, I urge you to go to www.authentichappiness.org , register and then take the test called VIA Survey of Character Strengths. VIA is an acronym for Values in Action. There are 240 questions and it takes about 25 minutes to complete. Be honest, and go with the initial answer that comes to mind. Try not to over guess an answer. Your child (ages 10 to 17) will complete the VIA Survey of Character Strengths for Children. These are free tests and have been published as a public service. The www.authentichappiness.org website, constructed by Dr. Martin Seligman, provides a number of validated self tests on the topics of positive emotions, engagement, meaning in life and life satisfaction. One test, the Brief Strengths Test, with only 24 questions, compares your results to others, broken down by people who took the test on the web, by gender, by age group, by occupational group, by education level and by zip code. The website is also a repository for evidenced based researchers and those interested in learning more about applied positive psychology. A newsletter about authentic happiness and announcements of initiatives in positive psychology that are seeking participants can also be found there. You might choose to participate in these initiatives at no charge. The website is a great resource!

To understand why identifying and using signature character strengths are important let's turn to the literature to determine what outcomes you can expect when you and your family members tap into their core character strengths. Signature character strengths are those character strengths you are naturally good at. People who are able to massage and exercise their signature strengths experience well-being, feel full of life, are more hopeful and have better health outcomes. Engagement with a signature character strength results in internal feelings of pride, satisfaction, joy, fulfillment and harmony. The display of a character strength does not diminish others around you but elevates and inspires them by seeing your passion for accomplishment. People who are authentic and at one in the world use their core strengths daily to produce abundant positive emotions. While there is at least one strength each person identifies very closely with, the signature strength, all people have a core of character strengths to draw from using different strengths or a combination of strengths based on the circumstances.

Determining virtues and strengths –the work begins

Charged with developing a scientific basis for positive psychology, Dr. Martin Seligman, Dr. Mihaly Csikszentmihalyi and an assortment of some of the most esteemed scientists on the planet examined characteristics shared by people leading the good life. Positive psychology takes a cross cultural, across time perspective. The building blocks to lasting happiness, overcoming depression or anxiety, generating well-being and leading the good or virtuous life are found in what positive psychologists discovered as common themes from major spiritual and philosophic literature. By studying virtuous themes explored by Aristotle, Confucius, Saint Thomas Aquinas, Bushido Samurai code, Bhagavad-Gita and many others, universal virtues were narrowed down to six that seem to apply to every culture. The six virtues identified are

- Wisdom and knowledge
- Courage
- Love and humanity
- Justice
- Temperance
- Spirituality and transcendence

Cultures support character strengths that embody these virtues through role modeling, institutions, rituals, parables, maxims, and children's stories like Grimm's Fairy Tales or the Wizard of Oz. Each of the virtues is realized through strengths of character.

When determining how a virtue is evidenced in the real world, a broad list of character strengths was generated and from that list, strengths were culled down to twenty four character strengths that were valued in almost every culture. These character strengths are valued in their own right and are tractable or adaptable, capable of being altered by outside forces. Here is the list of the twenty four strengths and their associated virtue.

Wisdom

    Love of Learning

    Judgment

    Curiosity

    Originality

    Perspective

Courage

    Integrity

    Bravery

Persistence

Vitality

Humanity and Love

Generosity and Kindness

Loving and Being Loved

Social/Emotional Intelligence

Justice

Teamwork

Fairness

Leadership

Temperance

Forgiveness and Mercy

Self Control

Humility

Prudence

Transcendence

Appreciation

Gratitude

Hope

Spirituality

Humor

You may be asking yourself can there really only be twenty four character strengths available to human beings? You may think one of your character strengths is not on the list. Dr. Alex Linley has developed a list of sixty strengths and believes that each individual has both realized and unrealized strengths, learned behaviors and weaknesses. For about $50.00 USD (Linley's website is in England so you pay in British pounds) you can take his Realise2 assessment. The website is www.realise2.com. I am neither recommending nor condemning of Linley's assessment tool. I have taken the assessment myself as part of my research for this book. You need to be the judge if you think there are strengths missing from the list above. You should feel completely in charge of your strength list and if you can't figure out where an unlisted core strength belongs in the taxonomy, create a category specific to you and place it under the appropriate virtue.

We cannot access our core strengths until we are challenged in our world. If you experience a character strength to its highest level and find easy evidence of its existence in your life, it would be one of your core strengths. How do you know if a strength is a core strength? You take ownership of the strength; it resonates with who you believe yourself to be in your essence. You have a rapid learning curve when you use the strength and excitement when challenges allow you to use the strength. When using the strength you get charged up instead of worn out. You often look for new ways to use the strength and gravitate toward projects where this strength can be exercised.

If you haven't taken the free VIA Survey of Character Strengths yet, go back and review the list of strengths and make a note of which of the strengths call out to you with greatest affinity and rank them on a scale of one to five, with one being the strength to which you feel most attenuated. Now look at the list again and select the five strengths you think are least like you. This exercise will help you understand the remainder of this section. If you took the VIA test on www.authentichappiness.org and didn't agree with the results, here is an opportunity for you to modify the core strengths the test ascribed to you and use your modified list - the top five strengths you think best describe you - for the rest of this section. You don't need to modify the five lowest ranked, just the five highest ranked.

Talents versus strengths

It bears repeating in this section that there are differences between talents and strengths. Talents are inherent to a person such as ability to sing, intelligence, athleticism. No matter how many singing lessons you take, even from the most gifted of teachers, if you don't have good pitch, you will still only be a nominal singer. On the other hand, strengths are cultivated.

Your child has a natural singing talent which is admired by many. She has the core strength of courage to allow her to share her talent publicly, even though she becomes anxious before each performance. The anxiety dissipates as soon as the first notes leave her vocal chords. She feels energized throughout the performance and this has a lasting positive effect for several hours after the performance.

Was it her talent or her strength that charged her up? While her talent is shared with the audience, her courage gave her the charge, boosted by the audience acceptance of her performance. Each of us is born with talents as part of our nature. Because talents are genetically inheritable, it is no wonder that we see generational stars. That is not coincidence. Children of movie stars may have more contacts in Hollywood than children of professors in Providence but it is talent that ultimately lands them fame in their own right.

Strengths, on the other hand, are reinforced with each learning opportunity and each person has the capacity to develop these strengths. Some strengths come more naturally to us than others but through diligent practice you can become adept at folding your core strengths into daily activities. Recognizing and nurturing a set of strengths, competencies and virtues in your child leads to future mindedness, hope, better interpersonal skills, capacity for flow, faith and a strong work ethic. Rather than trying to fix the lowest strengths, the goal of this section is to help you build on and enhance core strengths.

Internally validate your core strengths

Now that you have identified your core strengths, I challenge you to designate a time when you can exercise your signature or top strength. Here are a few examples to get you thinking:

Wisdom: Love of learning – attend a lecture at a local library on a topic you love

Courage: Persistence – go to the gym on a day you really just want to laze around

Humanity and Love: Generosity – clean out a closet and donate the goods in person

Justice: Teamwork – get a petition signed by your neighbors for one of your causes

Temperance: Self-control – don't eat dessert when dining out with friends

Transcendence: Appreciation of beauty – attend a new exhibit opening at the museum

After engaging in an activity that accesses your signature strength, reflect on these questions.

> How did the use of my signature strength change my mood and thoughts about well-being?
>
> Did I experience flow when engaging in this activity? Did time pass quickly? Did I lose my sense of self and feel completely connected to what I was doing?
>
> Did the activity I chose seem easy or too hard for me?

If you answered yes to any of these questions, you have experienced how accessing and honoring a core strength can be used to improve the quality of your life. You may want to go down the list of your top five to compare the outcomes when completing an activity that ignites each of your core strengths. After you have experienced this, work with your child so that he too may understand the importance of accessing and using core strengths.

In real world applications, avoid limiting yourself to engaging in activities that only fall in your core strengths or on a single core strength. You may discover latent strengths that, with practice, also enhance your well-being. Strengths are contextual and the number that you draw from at any given time is situational.

Strengths are not static; they are highly dynamic. While character strengths define a person and her response to the world, character itself is composed of an array of strengths. Core strengths are stabilizing influences in our lives but can change over time due to some strengths being underutilized. Strengths are interdependent, it's hard to isolate a single strength and try to use it exclusively to solve a problem, complete a task or build well-being.

> You promised your child you would finish the basement and let her move downstairs when she turned sixteen. You started the project but then got laid off from your job and were out of work for two months. Work stopped on the project. When you found a new job, the pay was 20% less than your previous job. Six months later you got a salary increase and you were able to afford to finish the basement. When you help your child move into her new room, you both experience the strengths of "appreciation" and "integrity". Your child experiences "gratitude" and you experience "persistence" and "generosity".

Core strengths can be limiting and have negative outcomes when we fail to stretch into other underutilized strengths. A child whose signature strength is curiosity can act unknowingly against her own self-interest if she over utilizes curiosity. To use an adage, curiosity killed the cat! Help your child recognize when to capitalize a core strength and when to dip further down the list of her strengths as she approaches an activity. No matter how far down the list prudence is, it is the best choice for some situations.

Lifting barriers to accessing our core strengths

Sometimes your child will not seem to be able to find activities, environments or challenges that activate her core strengths. Several barriers that have been identified in the scientific literature include not accepting or believing that positive feedback about a core strength is earnest or accurate, comparing herself to others without regard for observing that others are operating out of a different core strength set, having a fixed mindset (helplessness), failing to broaden and build emotional well-being, not challenging an unanticipated outcome, and failing to create habits to reinforce and reflect her core strengths.

To lift those barriers for your child give very specific positive feedback, with supporting and irrefutable evidence that she is operating within her core strength field and has demonstrated mastery as a result. Be a positive role model by acknowledging when you use your core strengths. Observe and report to your child when you have a positive emotional experience as a result of tapping into a core strength to accomplish a challenging task. Model a growth mindset, one that is not fixed on limitation. Recognize when your child has demonstrated a core strength by labeling the strength and the outcome as a result of using his known core strength. Encourage your child to act outside his comfort zone to surface underutilized or unrealized strengths and help him elevate those strengths into his core strengths. Refuse to let your child focus on perceived deficits, countering each defect with an alternative outcome if he uses his core strengths. Offer examples of problem solving strategies by using his core strengths.

Let's break down each of the strengths and look at qualities and considerations for each one. This section is formatted to first introduce you to the characteristics of the strength, evidence that supports whether this is a core strength for you, de-motivators and barriers to fully expressing the strength and thus gaining optimal positive emotions when the strength is expressed, and types of activities that encourage the use of the strength.

The Strengths defined

Wisdom – acquiring and using knowledge

Love of Learning

Internal motivational orientation is central to a love of learning. Information is gathered, synthesized and internalized just for the sake of the learning experience. Those who have a love of learning as one of their core strengths are charged up when they are allowed to learn new things on their own. Instructional settings such as school, workshops and laboratories that permit choice of learning style are ideal environments for a child to expand well-being. Where ever there is an opportunity to learn, the person with this core strength will thrive there.

You have evidence that curiosity is a core strength because you gain high positive feelings about learning and take on challenges with enthusiasm. You exhibit high resourcefulness and massage ideas, concepts and activities with an emphasis on gaining additional insight and information. You have a growth oriented rather than fixed oriented mindset when it comes to learning. You experience greater success in school and work as well as better emotional health when this strength is activated.

Love of learning can be inhibited when extrinsic rewards are attached to learning skills or information gathering because it is the internal drive that satisfies a learning lover. Learning in a high stress environment or under pressure reduces the amount of positive emotion derived from activating this strength. Being told you are doing something the wrong way (when actually it is just a different way of doing it) decreases the amount of positive emotional experience attached to learning something new. If you are asked to complete a novel task and are interrupted just as you are beginning to understand how to complete the task, and another takes over to complete the task for you, you likely experience negative emotions.

To encourage activation of this strength in young children, ask for their opinions, and talk about their feelings and the relationship between feelings and actions. Let your child make choices. Read to them at least fifteen minutes every day and ask your child what she learned and how it changes what she has previously known (knowledge integration). As children age, ask them to read to you as well. Start a book of the month club with older children who possess this core strength and, as a family, discuss the book after every one has completed it. Children with a love of learning will take more risks if you articulate your observation about how they approached a learning situation and what happened as a result of their style of learning. Encourage hobbies and mental pursuits that allow for research. A great topic at the dinner table for those who love to learn is for each family member to disclose one new thing he or she learned today. It is a brief but highly reinforcing activity for the learning lover in your family. Those with a love of learning prefer to learn by doing rather than being taught.

It is time to teach your daughter how to try her shoes herself or your son needs to learn how to tie his own tie. Instead of approaching it by saying "I am going to teach you how to tie your shoes today" you might say "I think you are ready to learn how to tie your shoes by yourself. What do you think?" If the answer is no, ask your daughter when she will know that it is time to learn how to tie her shoes for herself and create a list that you can hang on the wall. Check off the items on the list until she agrees that it is now time to tie her shoes by herself. When the answer is yes, you might say something like "This is how I tie my shoes. I am going to show you three times how I do it and you can follow along if you want. Then I am going to let you try to do it by yourself. If you want any advice on how I tie my shoes, I'll be glad to give it to you."

Using "I" statements and demonstrating the technique you use but not imposing a "right" way to tie shoes or a necktie allows your daughter or son choice, control and an opportunity to teach themselves something new.

Judgment

Open mindedness leads to better critical thinking and making judgments about the best course of action to take. Open mindedness gives a person permission to change their mind, take contrary evidence into consideration and determine when one's beliefs should be revised. Open mindedness reduces bias, pre-judgment and prejudice. Open mindedness leads to critical thinking while closed mindedness leads to non-critical thinking. Non-critical thinkers believe that their current belief is the only valid one, their perspective is the only sensible or reasonable one and their goal is the only valid goal. Critical thinkers learn a complex combination of core skills that include observation of the belief, interpretations of that belief, analysis of all the variables that impact that belief, inferences that can be made from all the evidence and an evaluation of the most reasonable course, given all the evidence. Critical thinking is comprehensive and exhaustive and ignores self-interest and emotional impulses. Critical thinkers tend to be skeptical, active thinkers. Critical thinking leads to judgment. Judgment as a strength is not related to judging someone against your own belief system (bias) or affiliation with a group that believes other groups are inferior (prejudice). Judgment is driven by reason over emotion after examining all the facts.

You have evidence that judgment is a core strength because you feel compelled to examine all the facts before drawing a conclusion. You don't take things on face value. You appreciate the perspectives of others and seek it out. You are willing to question your own beliefs or attitudes if you have facts that contradict them. You find it easier to "agree to disagree" than to defend your own thoughts and feelings to someone with a fixed mindset. Your decisions yield positive emotions because you are secure in the fact that you did not jump to a conclusion or make a snap judgment.

> Your child wants to ask a girl at school to attend the homecoming game and dance with him but he is reluctant to invite her because his best friend has also expressed an interest in inviting this girl to the game. He is afraid that the friendship will be damaged if he takes action. He hasn't talked it over with his friend and has not developed a pros and cons list of why he should talk it over with his friend. You encourage him to talk to his friend, examine all the evidence and then take appropriate action.

Open mindedness is inhibited by the way ideas are presented to us and the amount of time pressure we have to draw a conclusion and act on that conclusion. Critical thinking is influenced by the degree of open mindedness we have about the problem or belief. The outcome of taking a course of action is determined by our sound judgment once we have taken the most logical and unbiased course of action by critically thinking about the issue. We are more open-minded when incompatible goals are strong and conflicting.

To develop this strength, set up opportunities for your child to investigate, weigh the pros and cons and draw a conclusion based on the information he has collected. Talk with your child about the consequences of each action on his pros and cons list. Help your child reflect on his belief system about how the world works and challenge him to expand it. Offer copious opportunities to learn about different cultures and lifestyles to expand his world view. Create a safe space for you and your child to have well researched open debates about meaningful topics (as opposed to having arguments about his disappointment over a decision you have made that affects him.) Allow other family members to judge the veracity and relevance of the statements and select a winner at the end of the debate. Encourage your child to talk to a classmate that he wouldn't normally talk to about something that is happening at school to get a different viewpoint.

Curiosity

If your child always seems to be in discovery mode, exploring her physical, educational and thought worlds she is in touch with the strength of curiosity. She is open to new experience, has varied interests and actively seeks stimulation to counter boredom. She has an active desire for more information. A young child who frequently asks "Why?" may be expressing emerging curiosity and her naturally inquisitive nature.

You have evidence that curiosity is a core strength because you react positively to new, strange or mysterious stimuli. Likewise, if some element in the environment engages you, you explore it or feel compelled to manipulate it in some way and have a desire to know more about that element. You seek out new experiences and persist in your exploration of that experience until you close the information gap and figure out what you wanted to know. Once figured out, you quickly move on to find new things to be curious about. Curiosity typically arises spontaneously and is short lived, once the object of interested has yielded a satisfactory conclusion.

You child seems to love astronomy and has been asking about getting a telescope for two years. He is on a mission to see a list he is collecting of planets and constellations. The family goes to the planetarium at least once every other month and he has been able to use the planetarium telescope to see several of the planets on his list. He reminds you that the planetarium shows are just a simulation of the objects in the sky and feels driven to explore the night sky with his own eyes. You get him a telescope which he uses every clear night to find the objects on his list. You notice that he has not searched for the objects he has already seen through the telescope. Once his list is completed, he rarely uses the telescope and seems to have little further interest in astronomy. His curiosity has been satisfied and he moves on to other interests.

We often negatively reinforce the strength of curiosity, especially in very young children. Our motivation is almost always to protect them when we make statements like "don't touch that", "don't put that in your mouth" or "don't play in the street." As the child gets older she becomes very inquisitive, asking non-stop questions. It is easy after a long day at work to simply ignore most of the questions, especially if her questions are fueled by merely casual or idle curiosity and not related to knowing more about the world she is growing up in. "Why does a spider have eight legs?" is less likely to get a formal response than "why do some parents get divorced?" Schools teach children to get answers right on an exam rather than becoming curious about the subject matter. A child is often given explicit instructions along with an expected outcome. The child is not rewarded for being curious about what lies beyond the explanation he is expected to memorize. When limitations are imposed on harmless exploration, those who have the strength of curiosity don't get to practice this strength very much. Older children and adults who practice all-or-nothing thinking, who believe they already know as much as they want to know about a subject or have fears that knowing more about something will lead to harm suppress curiosity.

Giving a child with high curiosity needs the support he needs is challenging. Nonetheless, curiosity is painful if not satisfied. Curiosity exists for its own sake and there is no product that results when curiosity is satisfied beyond a better understanding of the object of curiosity. Curiosity is transient and superficial, intrinsically motivated and is expressed by desire to interact with the object of curiosity. Curious people like puzzles, riddles and problems to solve so allow for an ample supply of curiosity inducing games for the curious person. When your curious child asks questions, take time to answer them with appropriate and adequate responses. A child with low curiosity may be satisfied with "because I said so" but a child with high curiosity will continue to ask the same question until his curiosity is satisfied. Building on the curious child's sense of well-being can be helped by asking open-ended questions, where information is easy to obtain, well defined and where others your child knows already have the answer. If your curious child asks why spiders have eight legs, you could tell him that that's a great question and invite him to use the computer to look up the answer. You could ask what he thinks the answer is and then challenge him to verify his answer as correct or not. Curious children seek out a lot of variability in the environment; allow them to explore safely.

Originality

People who have this strength have a higher level of creativity than others, often expressed as what is called everyday creativity. People with "street smarts" show a lot of originality in how they behave socially. The way they approach the world is original and adaptive to the environment. While curiosity, once satisfied, quickly dissipates, creativity results in some product that is a positive contribution to the family, the community or the world-at-large. These products may include solutions, art or tangible products that are original and worthwhile. Creative people tend to have a higher tolerance for ambiguity and are curious by nature.

There are systematic steps to using creativity productively. First the idea is introduced and the mind begins preparing for the production stage in a variety of ways. The idea percolates down into the unconscious mind and lurks about until an "Aha!" or eureka moment occurs and the activities required to materialize the product become clear to the conscious mind. Finally, the creative person moves into the production stage and a product is realized.

You have evidence that originality is a core strength because you observe that you get excited about brainstorming a problem. You like improvisation such as creating, inventing, composing or performing with little to no advanced preparation. You quickly reframe problems and find solutions.

There is evidence that there is a neurobiological component to creativity and that creative persons are able to modulate neurotransmitters in the brain that stimulates the part of the brain responsible for creativity. Creativity is heightened when a person is in a supportive environment. Creative people enjoy having several simultaneous projects so that while one is incubating, another can be realized through the product. Creativity is stifled when a person is put under pressure to perform, is closely supervised on the project or when someone is consistently critical of the creative process.

At home your child is creative and expressive. He loves all kinds of arts and crafts and spends as many hours creating things each day as you will allow. When he tires of one activity he moves on to another and comes back later to the one he stopped. It may take him days to finish a project but you have many wonderful examples of his works of art displayed in your home. One day you get a call from the art teacher asking for a conference because your child is failing in art class. You find it hard to believe when you are informed that your child is anxious in art class, that he is failing because he doesn't show interest in the task, that he appears to have low participation and that he rarely turns in a completed assignment. Many of the art projects the teacher assigns are the kinds of activities your child loves to do at home. You talk to your child about the incongruence and find that he feels like he has no choice in what activity he can do, projects are time limited and have to be turned in by the end of class and that he is judged on his performance.

There are many ways to support the development of the strength of creativity in your family. First, help your child build basic skills about something she is interested in. The more information she has about something, the more creative she can be. Encourage "expert level" knowledge on subjects your child is interested in. Stimulate and reward curiosity and exploration by building internal motivation for learning and exploring. Help your child focus on age appropriate self-completion of projects to help her gain mastery of the strength and gain overall confidence by taking risks. Provide opportunities for choice and discovery. Find evidence of your child's mastery of creativity and point it out to her.

Perspective

For the purposes of this discussion, think of perspective as personal wisdom. Having perspective is to have a point of view. Points of view range from rigidly narrow to expansively broad. The broader one's perspective, the more wisdom they exhibit. Wisdom requires a deep understanding of the topic at hand. To experience wisdom we must often control our emotional reactions to the topic. Wisdom requires knowing what is true, based on a preponderance of evidence, and making a judgment of the right course of action based on those truths. Acting without wisdom causes adverse outcomes, negative emotions and suffering in life. Wisdom requires introspection and self-knowledge about what is valued in your life. When you activate wisdom, you are deliberately using your knowledge and experience to improve your well-being.

You have evidence that perspective is a core strength because you frequently check-in with yourself to articulate who you are as a person and how that will impact your actions. You have a strong drive for self-knowledge and use that knowledge to guide your decisions. You are genuine and direct in all your relationships. You ask other people you consider wise for advice. When asked for advice, you assist others in their own self discovery process. You are self-aware, self-conscious and have a well formed self-concept. Your actions are always consistent with your ethical beliefs and you acutely see the relationship. You pursue self-improvement to enhance well-being and reduce uncertainty about living a virtuous life.

Barriers to using perspective as a core strength include your present perception, your recollections of the past and your future predictions. You may have a misperception about a current event that you have not yet thought about critically. You may be misremembering the past which is frequently true for children when they say to you "You never let me go out with my friends." You may be predicting the future based on past experience and fail to act as a result. You may be over engaging in social comparison by comparing your well-being against someone you admire and being envious of that. When you abandon your moral principles, fail to act mindfully or with compassion or have insight without action, you are creating barriers to using perspective.

> You have allowed your child to go out with friends to celebrate his birthday with an agreement that he be home before six PM so that he can also celebrate his birthday with the family. He fails to get home until almost 7 PM. The reason for his lateness is that his friends wanted to see a movie that did not end until 6:30. Your child tells you that while the movie he and his friends intended to see ended at 5:30, when they got to the theatre they selected a different movie and he did not want to disappoint them. You help him understand that he made a commitment to the family

and that his wisdom would have helped him be more assertive and stand up to his friends.

To trigger perspective in your child, help her become more introspective by examining her thoughts, impressions and feelings. When she tells you she is having negative emotions, check-in with her about her self-perception and the causal relationship between self- perception and an outcome. When your child discloses she is having positive emotions after an outcome, talk with her about her self-concept and self-esteem and ask if her wisdom caused the positive emotions and led to the desired outcome. Frequently ask her to tell you about who she is as a person, what her values are and why those values are important. Support her as she considers the short and long term consequences of an action, the impact of that action on her well-being, the well-being of her family, close associations and society at large and how this action will align with her value system. Help her become aware of values and then offer alternative values based on varying situations. Remind her that perspective is having the deepest possible knowledge of the world and human nature and these are the determinants for right action.

Courage – accomplishing goals in the face of opposition

Integrity

People with integrity are authentic, genuine and honest. They speak the truth and live their lives accordingly. They are down to earth and without pretense. A pattern of truthfulness leads to honesty and a pattern of honesty leads to integrity. Truthfulness builds trust and families who value honesty are more open to each other and have higher well-being. Being honest is a morally courageous and difficult act at times but people whose signature strength is integrity find they lead highly authentic and satisfying lives. People who have integrity as a core strength choose truthfulness over deceit and believe they have a duty and obligation to not be deceptive.

Honesty and integrity can only be built when telling the truth is consistent and across all domains of a person's life. There are two forms of honesty, overt and covert. Overt honesty is making a conscious choice about whether to tell the truth or not and moving forward with a truthful answer. Covert honesty is expressed through our faithfulness, diligence, and dependability. Integrity is subjective; there are no predefined sets of universal absolutes. Integrity can only arise when we consistently adhere to our known values and our moral and ethical principles. People with high integrity take responsibility for their actions and hold themselves accountable for the actions they take. People with low integrity display dishonesty routinely, try to rationalize their responses and are impulsive in their actions.

You have evidence that integrity is a core strength because you steadfastly maintain your ground even as others attempt to violate your values and ethics. People seek out your perspective because they know you will give a straightforward answer. You don't hesitate to tell the truth in a respectful way, even if you know it may be painful. You don't keep secrets and you are authentic in everything you say. You never tell white lies. You would never dream of exaggerating an accomplishment and you always give full credit to others who assisted you in reaching a goal. You never lose sleep over something you were not forthcoming about. You never think about violating your own values.

Integrity is a skill that must be practiced and the benefit is not immediate or always apparent. For this reason, people who don't seem able to make integrity a core strength slip away from their values and become less honest. If it is beneficial to us or others, it is easy to be truthful. If it is a difficult truth to hear, concealing the truth to shelter oneself or another may seem to be a quick way out. Being secretive or hiding information from someone in order to protect them banishes the positive emotions generated by integrity. Top barriers to incorporating integrity into your life include your own defensiveness when another makes truthful observations that are painful, a fear of a negative consequence for telling the truth or trying to be "politically correct" in a situation. Not sharing feelings, disappointments, desires, dislikes, likes, hurts, anger, failures or needs is dishonest if not sharing these harms the family. Fear is at the root of not being truthful. Some of the fears related to dishonesty are fear of becoming exposed and vulnerable, fear of losing closeness or being abandoned because you are truthful, fear of being controlled once the truth is revealed, fear of judgment or fear of being challenged about your self-concept.

Your child tells you he landed an important role in the school play. He tells his friends at church and in the neighborhood he is the star. When you help him practice his lines, you notice there are only two lines for him to memorize. You point out to him that, while he is in the play, it is not a leading role. Nonetheless, he persists to his friends that he is the star performer. One of his classmates questions whether two lines makes him a star and he stops talking to this classmate. When the play is launched, his friends see that he is not the star at all. He is ridiculed in the neighborhood for exaggerating the truth. You have an opportunity to talk to him about dishonesty and the consequences from a real life experience.

A first step to making honesty a priority to your family is to make it one of your family values and a family rule, with consequences listed in your Family Charter. Talk to your child at an early age about the value of family honesty. Model honesty for your child. Build honesty by approaching your child calmly when they have been untruthful to make it safe for your child to be truthful. Acknowledge your appreciation of their courage to be honest even if you intend to attach a consequence for their dishonest behavior. Don't tell or tolerate "white lies." Harmless as they may seem, research has shown that exaggerating or telling white lies in the home without being confronted can lead to telling bigger lies at school. One study demonstrated that parents who recognize dishonesty and do nothing about it by either not questioning their gut about the veracity of the statement or simply ignoring it led to covert behavior in teenage boys including engaging in secretive behavior and criminal activity.

Bravery

While valor is defined as determined strength of mind or spirit in the face of danger to achieve a goal, bravery is assigned the characteristics of boldness, fearlessness and fortitude. Both valor and bravery are closely associated with the virtue of courage. Yet what we consider as bravery isn't always virtuous. Pirates are usually considered brave but they don't act in a virtuous manner when they plunder and pillage. Brave people do not shrink from challenge, difficulty, threat or painful experience but speak up for what is right even in opposition. Brave people act on their convictions.

When we talk about bravery in this section, we are talking about courageous bravery. Children view bravery as an action state while adults define bravery as exposing oneself to risk or injury. Bravery is the ability to confront fear and uncertainty, place oneself in danger, risk attempts to be intimidated and be willing to accept a painful outcome.

There are four types of bravery. Physical bravery is rare and puts us in the position to lose our lives. Running into a burning building to rescue a child is an example of physical bravery. Moral bravery, often referred to as moral courage, allows us to act on our convictions and values in the face of opposition or discouragement. We have many opportunities to practice moral bravery. Social bravery brings a group of people together to stand up for an unpopular cause, because they believe the status quo is unjust, knowing that each participant has an equal chance of being harmed as a result of the protest. Psychological bravery is the most personal of the four and it helps us overcome negative habits like recovering from substance abuse, being immobilized by irrational fears, refusing to participate in harmful relationships or releasing ourselves from negative past emotional experience.

Your child has been experimenting with alcohol with several of his friends for three months. One night you smell alcohol on his breath and confront him. He lies and tells you he has not been drinking. The following week, you smell alcohol on his breath again and confront him. This time he tells the truth but adds that it is the first time and accuses you of inducing him to drink because of your previous confrontation. "I figure if you are going to accuse me of drinking, I might as well see what drinking feels like", he retorts. You express concern and tell him if he has a problem, he can talk to you about it and together you will figure out what to do. He says there is no problem and promises not to drink again. The following week you get a call from one of his friend's parent who tells you that your son was at his house earlier and that the alcohol in the house had been consumed. When your son arrives home, you confront him and tell him you believe he has an alcohol problem and that you think he needs treatment. He reveals that he drinks almost every day and agrees to accept treatment.

You have evidence that bravery is a core strength because you consistently stand up for what you believe even if it means standing up alone. You don't cave in to pressure. Even when you are afraid you might fail, you try new things. You are known to express yourself even if others might disapprove when you feel strongly about an injustice. You stretch yourself to go on, even in the face of adversity. You know yourself well and examine your life often in order to improve it.

Barriers to mobilizing bravery include unconfronted self-doubt and giving in to fear. Staying in your comfort zone reduces your ability to practice bravery. People who don't trust their intuition may feel cowardly rather than brave. People who try to control outcomes don't activate their bravery skills. Not getting the outcome you want when you engage in an act from your brave self, reduces the willingness to practice bravery again. Acting out of reflex or fanaticism does not constitute bravery because they are acted upon impulsively and are based on moral reasoning and not moral courage.

Trusting your brave self requires a significant amount of practice before it becomes habituated into a core strength. There are five conditions to experience a morally courageous outcome. First you must recognize that you have been confronted with a moral situation. Second you have to recognize that you have a choice to act on this realization. Third, you determine the action that must be taken to correct the moral injustice. Fourth, you take individual responsibility for the outcome, even when you are involved in an act of social bravery. Fifth you must face the fear and determine that tolerating the fear is worth the potential outcomes.

For young children story telling about brave people and heroes and role playing bravery scenarios are effective in reinforcing the core strength of bravery. Helping your young child reach down to the brave self and sleep without a night light is one example of teaching bravery. Facing fears and taking risks are ways to teach older children about becoming naturally brave. For adults, raising personal standards and stepping out of your comfort zone causes positive emotions related to bravery. Help your child determine reasons to step out of their comfort zones and challenge her to go even one step further than she had imagined. Support your child in building confidence, a necessary ingredient for building bravery, by participating in courageous acts.

Persistence

People who have a signature strength of persistence are seen as industrious, diligent, and persevering. In order to persevere at a task, a person must be willing to overcome desires to give up and pursue an easier task. People who persist are able to risk lowering self-esteem temporarily to achieve a goal. They believe they can eventually accomplish the task. They do not cave in to discouragement from others or to external obstacles. Persistence is directed toward actions, beliefs and missions. Persistence is often met with sub-failures and highly persistent people take the experiences of the failure, learn from it and develop new strategies for success.

People with persistence as a core strength finish what they start, get assignments and tasks accomplished timely, don't get distracted from their desired outcome, take satisfaction in a job well done and remain goal directed despite the obstacles. When persistence pays off, a person with high persistence as a core strength gets charged up. There is an expectation that you will gain enjoyment of future goals and tasks when mastery is attained from a previous task requiring persistence. Persistence increases resourcefulness and skills related to the task. Persistence increases self-determination and self-efficacy. While people expect to be rewarded for persistence, these rewards are intrinsic. There is evidence that supports the fact that persistence decreases when the reward is external. Paradoxically people persist at tasks for a longer time when they have been told the task is difficult as opposed to easy.

While persistence is a highly successful strength for conquering difficult problems and activities, persistence is sometimes maladaptive and actually works against a person with this core strength. People with high persistence may work against themselves if they don't periodically evaluate the outcome based on the persevering efforts. Walking mindlessly and blindly down the same path without careful evaluation leads to maladaptive persistence. You need to stop persisting when it damages your well-being, when you acknowledge that there are barriers that you do not have the power to lift, when you recognize that your persistence is chasing after a wishful hope not based on facts or when your time, energy and other resources are greater than the realistic outcome you can expect based on facts. Persistence is a habit and a choice. You determine when it is constructive or destructive and persist or let go accordingly.

> You and your neighbor have children that are three months apart in age. Both have exhibited persistence as a core strength. They grew up together and were inseparable, enjoying the same activities, sports and interests. They attend the same schools and when your child enrolled in middle school, he and his friend tried out for the baseball team. Your child was selected but his friend was not. You notice that your child's friend has become withdrawn, tries to pick fights with your child, teases him in front of his peers and says cruel things about your child behind your child's back. He spreads vicious lies about your child. Your child

minimizes what is happening and its impact on his well-being and self-esteem. Your child steadfastly believes that his friend will come around and continues to invite him to do things and be friends. He has had earnest talks with his friend about how he wants to heal the relationship but the friend tells your child he will never forgive him. This behavior continues for several years. Nonetheless, your child persists in trying to repair the friendship. Nothing works but your child keeps persisting. Your child starts becoming anxious and even tries to fail at a few things to show his friend he will sacrifice success to reclaim the friendship. He tries to drop out of baseball but you convince him to continue on the team. Your child's well-being is suffering and he spends more and more time trying to figure out what he hasn't tried. He has even violated his integrity to win his friend back. It's time to have a conversation with your child about the negative effect of persistence and help him rigorously examine the path he is taking and its doomed ending.

You have evidence that persistence is a core strength because you never give up on the things you think you can accomplish. You take great pride in yourself when you accomplish difficult tasks but the pride is self-bestowed. You embrace difficult tasks and stand up for what you believe. Even when tasks are really hard or really boring, you complete them to gain that sense of accomplishment. You accept initial failures without getting so disappointed you look for an easier task to accomplish. You may occasionally chase a fantasy but stop when you realize the end result you wanted is hopeless.

Barriers to practicing and building up your capacity for persistence are both physiological and psychological. Persons diagnosed with developmental disorders or mental retardation exhibit less capacity for persistence when placed in clinical studies on persistence. Those persons with a diagnosis of ADHD have higher distractibility than the public at large and distraction gets in the way of persistence. In clinical studies, those living with a diagnosis of depression are seen to give up more easily than those who have not been diagnosed with depression. The desire to reduce anxiety can lead to giving up more easily when the desired goal raises anxiety to high levels of discomfort. People active in their substance use disorder demonstrate lack of self–control and increased impulsivity, both of which contribute to the inhibition of persistence.

Having a pessimistic explanatory style (see the section How to Foster a Flourishing Family to review explanatory styles) or unrealistic expectations of an outcome (continuing to persist despite knowing there is no successful outcome) leads to low persistence tolerance. People with low self-esteem don't persist if persistence is perceived as a threat to self-esteem. High procrastinators and those with a lack of intrinsic motivation to complete a difficult task also do poorly on persistence tests. When intrinsic motivation (success for success's sake) is replaced with an extrinsic reward (reward for reward's sake), persistence diminishes. People with low self-awareness attribute failure to self-ability rather than outside influences or lack of trying hard enough. This results in giving up and trying an easier task rather than persevering and looking at alternative ways to approach the problem.

Persistence is a choice and must be practiced regularly before it becomes a habit. Acknowledging examples of where persistence paid off (or didn't) helps your child recognize the attributes and outcomes of practicing persistence. Encourage a can-do spirit and don't rescue your child when the going gets tough. Young children learn about persistence from stories such as The Hare and Tortoise, Three Little Pigs and The Little Train That Could. Persistence is hard to articulate for younger children. Consider helping your child make a poster of various "I can do it", 'Don't give up", "The fight has just begun" and other meaningful statements she can think about when she feels frustrated by a difficult task. Help your older child think about the future and imagine the feelings she will get when the task is accomplished. Have you child ask others how they persevered through a difficult class or being bullied if your child is facing the same thing. At a challenging time for your child, explore with her any negative thoughts or situations she might use to discontinue the project and how she will counter those thoughts or situations. Remind her she has a choice to stay committed and ask her what she needs from herself to stay on course.

Vitality

Zest, passion and vigor all describe qualities of vitality. People with vitality as a core strength are seen by others to relish life and be lively. They exhibit an abundance of physical and mental energy. They approach life with joy, passion and enthusiasm. They love to try out all sorts of new things, keep their health in balance and appear strong, energetic and robust. They have active minds and active bodies. While there are studies on physical, mental and emotional vitality, one can observe evidence of spiritual, social, intellectual, family and community vitality as well.

Physical vitality is having energy, stamina and enthusiasm. It includes physical wellness even if you have a disease or disability that prevents you from engaging in vigorous physical activity. Many studies show that people who are severely disabled often exhibit high levels of zest for life. Mental vitality is clarity of thought and a desire to put ideas together, represented by mental alertness and the mental stamina to think through problems completely.

Emotional vitality is your sense of well-being, resilience to the difficulties in life and a preponderance of positive emotions. Spiritual vitality is knowing what your spiritual values are and remaining true to them in your day to day life. Social vitality is a fearlessness of interacting in your social environments, both work and play, with other persons. Intellectual vitality is your thirst for information and how you put ideas together. Family vitality occurs when loving families support each other, enjoy common activities and feel a special spark when the family is together. Community vitality is when you feel fully involved in the community and the community supports each member. No matter the context, vitality is expressed by your enthusiasm to be connected and the positive emotions you store up by these connections.

You have evidence that vitality is a core strength because you experience enthusasm for most things, no matter how droll they may be. You see life as a marvelous adventure and you have a first class ticket. You typically feel full of energy and rarely experience fatigue or disinterest, no matter what the situation. Even if you are faced with difficult obstacles, you willingly accept the challenge and make the best of everything available to meet the challenge. If you have a debilitating health condition such as chronic pain or a life threatening illness, you adjust your life so you get maximal satisfaction given your limitations. You put your physical, mental and emotional well-being at the top of your list and look on the bright side. Others want to be around you because your passion brings them up with you.

What reduces the positive effects of vitality and a passion for living? From a personality perspective, neuroticism attacks the conditions of positive affect, energy and vigor – known to increase happiness and life satisfaction - and elevates fatigue and negative affect. Neuroticism, one of the "Big 5" Personality dimensions (the other four are openness, conscientiousness, extraversion and agreeableness) reduces vitality. Big 5 personality dimensions are generally accepted as being heritable, that is to say they can be passed on from generation to generation. People with high neuroticism as a personality dimension find it challenging to feel invigorated. Persons experiencing an episode of depression, bi-polar swings or anxiety have a diminishment of emotional vitality. While they may feel highly energized (positively or negatively), it is not the invigorating feeling that builds positive emotions. Trying to be what you are not reduces vitality. It takes a lot of energy to put up a façade but the disappointing outcome robs you of vitality. High levels of stress reduces physical vitality as does recent illness, pain, fatigue, poor diet, smoking, excessive alcohol or drug use and lack of regular exercise. Emotional vitality is compromised when a person feels he has lost his autonomy, he is in a strained relationship or he stops accessing activities that raise his spirit. Family vitality is diminished during times of family crisis. Community vitality is contingent upon the continued success of the community where you live. If there are foreclosures all around you, you will experience a loss of community vitality which contaminates your overall vitality and the vitality of your family. If you are eschewed by your social network, your vitality diminishes.

Pay attention to an area of vitality that is compromised and recognize that it has an effect on all areas of vitality. If your child is a high vitality person, allow his passion to move the family forward. For physical vitality, put your family on a "health-kick" plan that includes ample exercise and healthy eating habits. Vitality provides the highest positive emotional experience when each member of your family strives to be her best self, not her perfect self, her comparative self or her highest self.

Your family spends a lot of time together and all of you have vitality as a core strength. You go to the zoo, amusement and theme parks, the planetarium to see IMAX movies, the museum or a concert nearly every Saturday. You go out to dinner as a family routinely and include weekly rituals of "Mexican Monday" at your local Mexican restaurant and "Pizza Party Friday" at your favorite Italian place. Your family falls on hard financial times and you can no longer afford the outings. Meals are prepared at home. Everyone realizes that money is tight and that the family has to sacrifice. Over the coming weeks, you notice the children are withdrawing, spending more time at friends' houses, watching a lot of TV or playing computer games. You and your partner are beginning to bicker. You express you concerns about this behavior at a family meeting and help the family recognize that without the excursions and dinners out, you don't have a focus for family time, the very thing that kept everyone charged up. Your family decides to revive some of the rituals and now makes tacos together as a family on Mondays and Fridays become "invent a pizza night" where each member concocts a recipe for an unusual pizza you cook at home. Every month the family votes on who wins the "Pizza With Pizazz" award, and the winner gets to keep a small trophy you bought at the dollar store in their room until the next election. You pull the bicycles out of the shed and have a family bicycle adventure ride each Saturday, which includes a picnic in the free community park. Back on track, the family revitalizes and every member begins building positive emotions again.

Teach your child the transience of all experience. Let her know that she will not always feel positive emotions and that she will not always succeed. Even when she is set off track, your child can feel the zeal and passion for living. Teach your child to find activities, surroundings and experiences that help her feel strong, energetic, robust and active in mind, body and emotion. Ask her what motivates her and fills her with energy and enthusiasm. Make certain she has access to those experiences and environments. Encourage her to pay attention to how it feels in optimal conditions and how she plans to expand the conditions that reinforce her gusto for life. Family communication, family bonding and family connection all lead to an increase in positive emotions for those with a core strength of vitality.

Humanity and Love – strengths of befriending and tending to others

Generosity

Those who have this as a core strength are described by others as kind and generous, never too busy to help someone out in a time of need or doing good deeds for others, even if they are strangers. They conduct altruistic acts, acts that are unselfish in motive. For our discussion keep in mind that altruism, generosity and kindness are focused on the other and their benefit from our action, but we also get to bask in the byproduct of positive emotions after we have completed an act of kindness. There is evidence that altruism is associated with the Big 5 personality dimension of agreeableness, which has a hereditary predisposition. If you are generous, it is likely your genetics, combined with learning how to be generous from your family that has contributed to your capacity to be generous. Embraced concepts that describe a person with the core strength of generosity include compassion and nurturance of others. Your motivation is not self-satisfaction, per se, but eliminating suffering that others experience.

Persons who align with generosity as a core strength share a belief system that includes that everyone is equally important, despite their life circumstance or world perspective. They believe that giving is as important as receiving. They are convinced that people who are suffering need compassion and care. Doing good for others is a maxim by which people with this core strength live. Kindness extends beyond family and close associations and spills into the community and the world-at large. Persons with high generosity are pro-social and unlimited with regard to who they offer generosity.

You have evidence that generosity is a core strength because egoism is never a motive for being kind to others. You stop to help a stranger on the street even if they don't match your demographic. You shy from the limelight when others want to publicize your good deeds. You have a high empathy with others even if you cannot sympathize (I've been there and know what it is like" or "I haven't experienced this but I can imagine the experience vividly"). You have good moral reasoning, recognizing you get no direct benefit from what you are doing but knowing it still needs to be done. You feel affinity to social responsibility, believing you have a personal ethical responsibility to care for others.

Your child is on a walk from your neighborhood to the next neighborhood to visit a friend. They plan to watch a movie together and he is running ten minutes late so he is in a hurry. He passes a pond and sees an overturned bicycle and a person on the ground. Without regard for time, he quickly runs to the aid of bicyclist and discovers she is in pain and bleeding. He immediately calls 911 and comforts the victim until an ambulance arrives. He gives encouraging words to the victim and continues on his journey, arriving 45 minutes late for the movie. His friend has called you expressing worry because of the agreement to watch the movie from the opening credits. When your child arrives at his friend's home, he calls you to explain his lateness. Later in the evening the local news team calls to schedule an interview with your child about his heroic intervention. While your child never misses an opportunity to publicize his successes you get the response "That's ridiculous. I'm no hero. Someone needed to help and I was there to help her. I don't want to be interviewed. Let's tell the news team I have nothing to say." Your child's sense of responsibility, duty and loyalty has superseded his desire for fame.

Barriers to kindness, generosity or even altruism are often self-imposed. While altruism and the positive emotions associated with altruism are elevated by the agent of altruism and spill over to others who witness the altruism, altruism is not universal or unconditional. Being kind to all people, all the time, no matter what they have done leads a relatively unfulfilled existence and exposes one to feelings of being exploited. Being generous involves a level of sacrifice, even when it appears to be intrinsically motivated. Kindness and generosity to a bully does not encourage reciprocal kindness from a bully. One barrier to altruistic love (kindness or generosity) is focusing excessively on the means versus the ends. If the means, for example, are giving to a charity versus the ends, focusing on the goals of the charity and you only donate to the charity you are thwarting generosity and kindness or altruism. If you do not know deeply or care about others people's concerns, you are operating out of charity, not generosity. If you are promoting your individual expression and the motive is materialism over altruism, you derive no positive emotions from the act. Those divergent compelling motives to act supersede the outcome. Promoting status over shared opportunity is derisive. You are unsupportive in an altruistic way unless your concerns are supported by faith and determination in the future of the recipient. Excessive demands, both personal and situational, reduce your capacity to be genuinely generous. For example, your company expects you to support a charity so they can say they are at a 100% contribution level in the community for their charity drive. You give in and agree to a 10% reduction in your gross pay each pay period. This is not an expression of generosity, but of compliance, and does little to build positive emotions.

Other barriers to expressing generosity are more intractable. You or your child may not have the trait for generosity but conversely have a low disposition for generosity. You may not have natural empathy (but it can be learned) and you may have hedonic urges (satisfaction for self, fearing what you will lose if you help) over internalized urges to be of assistance to others. You, or your child, may have a low sense of social responsibility.

Teaching your child how to express generosity depends on a number of factors both genetically inherited and learned. If your child is predisposed to the genetic imprinting of altruism, kindness and generosity you may need to teach discernment. Knowing when to use this skill, and when to walk away, is essential to his physical and emotional well-being. Know that while easy to agree to altruism, it is hard to act on it when in the face of harm. Based on the evidence, action should be prevented. Whether or not agreeableness is a personality trait your child exhibits, there are many activities you can involve him in to teach generosity. Help your child identify positive moods when he is helpful around the house, supporting family or peers or expressing hope for a community or school success. Teach your child how to identify and express empathy. Know that there are many interventions to teach kindness found in parenting resources, mentoring activities and in the educational system. Take advantage of them. Young children are susceptible to observing that nurturing people, through modeling, leads to altruistic nurturing, based on research findings.

Counter physical and emotional insensitivity by giving an alternate viewpoint. Train your child to never harm others. Undermine his incompatible beliefs around discrimination and prejudice toward those who need assistance. Remind your child frequently that altruism is equivalent to a nobler nature and that generosity is a learned experience and doesn't come naturally to all people. Celebrate but don't reward altruism.

Loving and Being Loved

Love is the capacity to successfully attach to others and to allow others to successfully attach to you with authenticity, warmth and consistency. Love has cognitive, behavioral and emotional aspects. Love is attached to family and those we are very close to. Love from a child to a parent is strengthened when the child feels safe, knows the parent is there when the child needs her parent and the child misses the parent when the parent is absent. Love from a parent to a child is expressed by making the child feel safe, being available when the child needs the parent and letting the child know the child is missed when the child is absent. Romantic love is a passionate desire to attach to another adult so that you make each other feel safe, you have confidence that you are there for each other when it is needed and you miss each other when you are apart. Love is innate and provides survival for the species.

How we attach to others demonstrates our capacity to love and be loved. Dr. Mary Ainsworth, the pioneer of attachment theory, spent her career studying how people come to adopt an attachment style. It has been shown that securely attached infants in later life explore more, are more persistent in problem solving, and are more likely to ask for help when they need it. In school, securely attached children require less contact with teachers for guidance or discipline, display less attention seeking behavior, and have lower impulsivity, less helplessness, better frustration tolerance and better interpersonal skills. Adolescents and adults who were securely attached to an adult caregiver in infancy cope better with stress, develop stronger social ties and have better trust and intimacy with others. When attachment security is uncertain, people behave negatively in an attempt to get the other to respond to their attachment cues.

You have evidence that love is a core strength because you value and feel fully secure in your loving relationships. You express love unconditionally with sincerity, warmth and consistency. You feel close to those who feel close to you. You are willing to sacrifice for those you love. You know your trust and support needs are being met from those who love you. You feel a loss when those you love are absent for extended periods. You'll do almost anything for the ones you love. You freely allow others to offers expressions of love to you. You have unconditional positive regard for those close to you. You never feel insecure or jealous.

Barriers to gaining positive emotions from secure attachment are jealousy, insecurity and insensitivity. Lack of a well-recognized support system, poor communication and high levels of stress reduce the positive impact of love. Environments filled with conditional love, anger, abuse, prejudice, neglect or invoke shame or fear are not conducive to experiencing love. Barriers to secure attachment can be overcome at any age with proper attention to understanding the drivers of attachment.

There are four types of attachment styles described in the literature. Attachment style is influenced by an infant's experience of the caregiver. There must be at least one caregiver for an infant to develop a relationship with for social and emotional development to thrive. If the primary caregiver responds to the infant's needs promptly, reliably and with warmth for the first twelve months of the child's life, secure attachment begins to develop. According to attachment theory, responses from the caregiver during the first year of life form the basis of future relationships.

From birth to six months the caregiver must be consistently sensitive and responsive to the infant's needs. When the infant starts to crawl, the caregiver becomes the secure base from which the infant can explore the world and come back to following her exploration. At this age, separation anxiety is experienced when a securely attached infant loses sight of the caregiver but this dissipates as the child gets older. Around the age of six, attachment begins to transfer to peers and parents can identify the attachment style their child has adopted through those relationships. Full attachment transfer begins around adolescence.

Depending on the experience the infant had during the formative stages of infancy and young childhood, he will act out one of four attachment styles. Secure attachments (love and being loved) forms when the caregiver has acted appropriately. Insecure-avoidant attachment forms when the caregiver has been inconsistent or neglectful. Insecure-ambivalent attachment forms if the caregiver offered little or no responsiveness. Disorganized attachment forms when the infant was maltreated during the first year of life.

Adult attachment styles are identified as secure, anxious-preoccupied, dismissive-avoidant and fearful-avoidant. Securely attached adults are comfortable with intimacy and independence in their romantic relationships. They have positive views of each other and themselves. Anxious-preoccupied adults seek out high levels of intimacy but remain distrustful of their partners. They often become overly dependent on a partner to meet their needs. They worry about the relationship, are impulsive and have high levels of emotional expression. Dismissive-avoidant adults avoid close adult relationships, see themselves as highly independent and suppress feelings they have for their partner, whom they select often because they have a low opinion of the partner. Fearful-avoidant adults mistrust their partners and are afraid of intimacy. They are uncomfortable with close emotional relationships.

> Your partner comes home from work two hours late and is obviously intoxicated. You become enraged and scream in front of your two year old and five year old children that you feel abandoned. You ask what would have happened if you had stayed out late and came home drunk. You berate him for being irresponsible and tell him how you feel like you are always stuck with the kids and that you would like to have some fun too. You threaten that one day you are going to go out and come home drunk so he can see what that feels like. The next day you notice your two year old is anxious and your five year old is withdrawn. If your children continue to see this pattern of behavior, they will come to believe they are unsafe, that you will not be there when they need you and that there is only conditional love in your home. If you apologize to them for throwing a tantrum in front of them, assure them they are loved and that you want them in your life, you see a reversal of the anxiety and withdrawal

There is encouraging evidence that nearly all people, at any age can learn to form secure attachments with those they love. Practitioners of emotionally focused couples therapy have good results in helping willing couples build secure attachment to each other. If you and your partner are not securely attached, it is difficult for your child to learn what secure attachment (love) looks like. If your attachment style is anxious, dismissive or fearful, pay attention to the feelings that arise when you exhibit the characteristics of your attachment style. Identify the thoughts associated with those feelings and examine them. Have you had those feelings in the past? What triggered them? Is this the same experience repeating itself or are you using your attachment style to protect yourself from an undesired outcome? What do you predict the outcome to be if you change your attachment style and practice secure attachment skills (authenticity, warmth, consistency)? If your child is exhibiting poor attachment, ask him what he needs he isn't getting around issues of safety, assurance that you are there when he needs you and that you miss him when he is gone.

Social/Emotional Intelligence

Social intelligence is knowing how to get along with others and emotional intelligence is knowing how to get along with yourself. It requires the ability to identify, assess and control your emotions and how the emotions and actions of others are impacted through your awareness of their emotions. Social/emotional intelligence is measured by how effectively you detect and understand your and others emotions, how well you understand how emotions can be manipulated and how you manage your emotions. People who have this signature strength are highly self-aware of their emotions, drives, values, goals, strengths and weaknesses. They engage in self-regulation of their feeling states and are able to adapt quickly when their feelings begin to overwhelm them. People with high social/emotional intelligence are adept at managing relationships and exhibit high empathy. Their motivation for achievement is just for the sake of the achievement.

You have evidence that social/emotional intelligence is a core strength because you can easily read the emotions and values of others and use that information to get them to take action. You pay attention to feeling states and the environmental triggers related to each feeling state. You are not afraid to go with your gut feelings. You are unafraid to express your feelings to others and you want to know how they are feeling as well. You are highly empathic and express empathy often. You pay careful attention to what the other is saying and interpret non-verbal communication cues including facial expression, cadence of the conversation, postures, gestures, proximity and tone of voice while maintaining eye contact during conversations. You listen before you speak. You often use humor and play to deal with challenges. Despite difficult environmental demands and high pressure to accomplish a goal, you are successful in reaching your goals, and getting others to assist you in reaching those goals. You are unflappable.

People with low social/emotional intelligence typically experience a high degree of emotional dysregulation and are not able to control their feelings. They have impaired reality testing skills, are poor problem solvers, don't tolerate stress well and may have difficulty with impulse control. Several studies indicate that emotional intelligence scores go up when people stop using alcohol or drugs. People with low social/emotional intelligence are afraid to identify or express emotions because they believe that emotions are an obstacle, not a resource, to accomplishment. Engaging in distracting experience in order to avoid emotions is frequently seen in people with low social/emotional intelligence. They become confused when they have conflicted emotions.

Your child told a friend a secret and the friend betrayed her. She tells you her feelings "are over the place" and they are immobilizing her from taking action. The emotions are so strong she is avoiding her friend and her peer group. You help her sort out the feelings and determine she is mad at her friend, scared that her peers will find out the secret and sad this could have happened to her. As she begins to manage each feeling, and the triggers for those feelings, she maps out a course of action. She decides she will confront her friend and let her know she is hurt by her friend's action and that she forgives her but will be cautious about telling her secrets in the future, thus managing her anger in an emotionally intelligent way. She decides that since the secret is out, she will tell her peer group the secret so she doesn't have to feel scared they will find out. This is a healthy expression of social intelligence. She reflects on the experience and determines that she has gained self-awareness and better social skills and this reduces her sadness.

Activities to teach your child better social/emotional intelligence include learning about emotional regulation, discovering ways to quickly identify stress, offering ways to resolve conflicts with confidence and participating in mindfulness activities (described previously in the book.) Young children don't naturally regulate emotions very well but can be taught through modeling. When you child becomes upset, stay calm, validate the emotion, ask him to label the emotion with words, and give him some optional ways to frame his outcome. Older children can reduce emotional intensity by labeling the emotion, determining the reason they are experiencing the emotion and deciding what needs to happen to reduce the intensity of the emotion. Teach your child to observe how his body feels when he is stressed out so he can quickly reduce stress before it becomes overwhelming. Ask him how his breathing changes or if he gets any sensations in his body such as tingling, a sensation of a band around his head or butterflies in the stomach when he has an intense negative emotion. Ask him if his thoughts become more scattered or if he reduces the number of thoughts he has. Ask him to describe what it feels like in his body when the stress dissipates. Teach your child to observe others and start looking for the non-verbal cues listed earlier in this section. Explain the four stances to take when conflict arises if he wants to positively resolve a conflict with confidence. One choice is to confront the conflict while remaining in the present and refusing to focus on other past events even if they seem related. Another choice is to forgive the other person and move on. A third choice is to analyze the importance of the conflict and to choose his battles wisely. The fourth choice is to disengage, agree to disagree, and refuse to argue his case any further if the other person is unwilling to resolve the conflict. The most important thing to remember about Social/Emotional intelligence is that is a learned set of behaviors centered around learning to recognize and manage emotions and observing the impact of those emotions on the success of the activity.

Justice – strengths that build community

Teamwork

People for whom this is a core strength are not driven by self-interest but by a higher purpose. A high value is placed on good citizenship and loyalty to a cause bigger than oneself. They align with a group and desire to meet the obligations and responsibilities of that group. They are bound by duty to ensure the success of the group for the common good of all. They collaborate and cooperate with others to reach a common goal. They believe they have a social responsibility to act, not just comment, on a civic cause. They work hard for the success of the group over individual accomplishment. They are loyal to their country, their civic beliefs and their teams. The first inklings of loyalty for younger children may be loyalty to the family. As a child gets older, loyalty to a school, a religious institution the family belongs to, a charity the family volunteers to serve, a political cause the family believes in all represent opportunity to experience loyalty, teamwork and civic pride. As you see your child with teamwork as a core strength grow older, you can expect to witness expressions of identification and affiliation with a group to which he feels obligated to participate in for the common goals of that group. People with a core strength of teamwork and social responsibility exhibit higher levels of trust and a more positive view of human nature.

You have evidence that teamwork is a core strength because you love community involvement and feel obligated to participate. You are a loyal parent, friend and worker. You like to get involved in causes for the greater good. You volunteer for committee work. You prefer working on a group project over an individual project. You feel a strong duty to improve the human condition. You volunteer for your favorite political candidate, working tirelessly to get her elected. When you disagree with an action your group is taking, you speak up for the betterment of the group, not your individual preference.

Barriers to deepening this strength include not giving your child the right to express his views. When you don't involve your child in family decisions, you are teaching him that his opinion does not count. Not allowing your child to set his own priorities or ignoring his preferences, leads to poor social skills when he does become involved in "greater good" activities. If your child does not have control over outcomes in the home, he will be less likely to participate in civic activities. Parents who tell their child that he lacks competence or experience to inform a conversation about politics or policies stifle the creative spirit in their child. Telling your child you are not interested in his viewpoints does likewise. It is not about the child getting what he wants but being heard that he wants it.

Your child has an oppositional view to yours regarding an increase in the local sales tax in order to improve the parks in town. Your viewpoint is that there are enough taxes already and the parks, while not in excellent shape or having a variety of activities, are adequate the way they are. You and your family don't use the public parks and you think his interest is dramatic and silly. You refuse to discuss the matter with him. A group of his fellow-middle school classmates are forming a coalition to "Save Our Parks" and he asks to join it. You refuse, reminding him that he is too young to vote and expressing your doubt that this group will have any impact on the vote. You tell him you don't ever want to hear another word about this issue again. You have disempowered your son from learning about teamwork, social responsibility and civic pride. You have modeled that his opinion doesn't count. He stops talking about politics and civic duty.

To build a sense of belonging and desire to serve the greater good, family values should include compassion and empathy. These values play a key role in fostering social responsibility. Children need to see evidence of the positive outcome as a result of tending to community needs as well as family needs. Without this impression, your child cannot emulate that behavior and understand the concept of social responsibility. Teaching empathy at a very young age produces caring adolescents who exhibit concern for marginalized people and who contribute much to their community. Adolescents who are involved in at least one extracurricular activity have more positive views of others and become more trusting. Trust increases the likelihood that your child will become involved in civic activities, which leads to better well-being and a sense of belonging. Social trust is increased when your child is involved in charitable groups that have a diverse composition. Evidence suggests that social trust is not developed when your child joins homogeneous, self interest groups. Research indicates that youth from better educated families are more likely to become involved in civic activities and that youth who get involved in political groups tend to become more tolerant.

Fairness

Fairness is about treating people fairly and not letting personal bias stand in the way of fairness. People who have fairness as a core strength believe that everyone should get a fair chance. Fair people believe in equity and justice. Fairness is a product of moral judgment and is developed through moral reasoning so what is fair may seem different for different people based on their moral development. There are several generally recognized types of fairness in addition to moral fairness. A judgment about equity fairness is made when resources are divided among the recipients based on effort, ability and productivity. A judgment about equality fairness occurs when every recipient in the group receives an equal amount of a resource, without regard to effort, ability or productivity. Some businesses give an across the board pay raise to every employee, based on profits (equality). Then selected employees working for the business may get an additional increase based on reaching individual goals (equity). These definitions of fairness are oriented to economics.

The core strength of fairness described in positive psychology is the moral and ethical rightness or wrongness of an action. Fairness as a core strength is a mixture of moral judgment and thinking about how the action will impact you and others in your group. Dr. Lawrence Kohlberg, in his work on moral development believed that justice (fairness) is the essential characteristic of moral reasoning. Kohlberg identified six stages of moral development. The first is an obedience/punishment dichotomy, driven by the desire not to get punished. The second stage is driven by self-interest. The third stage is driven by interpersonal conformity, the fourth driven by law and order morality, the fifth by social contract (what you agree to as a member of your group) and the sixth is driven by universal ethics (people should not kill other people, apply the golden rule etc.) While people can get to the sixth stage, not all do. As a result, their ability to determine fairness is limited to the stages they have been able to integrate into their moral reasoning. Dr. Carol Gilligan contributes an additional element to moral justice and fairness and that is the factor of care. Care reasoning includes the needs and perspectives of others as well as our own in determining what is morally just and fair.

You have evidence that fairness is a core strength because you examine all the facts before rendering judgment about what is just. When you believe something is unfair, you speak up with cogent arguments about why you disagree. You don't look at justice as different for different people but that justice crosses all cultural lines and must be applied equally. You operate from a situational ethics perspective rather than taking a parochial viewpoint.

There are barriers to getting the most positive emotions from the core strength of fairness. These include failing to have a clear moral identity, failing to use perspective when determining fairness and low self-awareness. Moral problem solving is not innate and must be practiced, with outcomes examined, before this can become a natural process when looking at what is fair and what is not. A barrier to consistently and successfully using fairness to increase well-being may be faulty interpretations of distributive fairness (the outcome) or procedural fairness (the process to determine the outcome). If you don't have all the facts, it is difficult to draw a morally valid conclusion about an activity that is fair or unfair. If you believe you had no control over the process, you may have difficulty believing the outcome is fair. Inhibiting factors for a child's learning about moral reasoning and fairness is directly related to parenting style. A parent who acts against her own moral code teaches that fairness is not very important. Likewise a parent who is in the lower stages of moral development himself cannot model the higher stages of moral reasoning to his child. A child who lives in a household with little decision-making capability doesn't have opportunity to learn about moral reasoning. A child who experiences an authoritarian parenting style is not encouraged to think about fairness. A household that is more conflictual than emotionally supportive may find that their child has a harder time grasping the concepts of fairness.

Your child is learning about moral reasoning at school through an episode of games and stories. She tries to tell you about what she is learning about moral reasoning and judgment each night when you get home from work. You appear disinterested, because you are tired when you get home. Instead of talking it through with her, you dismiss her and tell here that you know the difference from right and wrong and you will teach her how to distinguish right from wrong. Two weeks later she disagrees with your interpretation about something you consider is just and fair. When she shares with you that she sees it differently, you cut her off and inform her that you know what is right and what is wrong. She questions you as to how you came to the conclusion you did. Your response is "Because I say it is." What have you taught your child about fairness?

Parents who have a child with fairness as a core strength can support this strength through parenting style. A child with this strength will be less disagreeable in the household where discussion based parenting takes place. Parents who have a child with fairness as a signature strength need to avoid the use of love withdrawal as a way to shape a child's behavior. Families who use the Family Charter system will never need to use love withdrawal. Teach the fair-minded child all you can about autonomy, commitment, respect and empathy. Reinforce your child's love to learn and help him seek out new challenges, especially intellectually stimulating challenges. Verbally acknowledge your child when you see evidence that he is taking reasonable risks or demonstrating self-responsibility. Help him make plans and set goals that go beyond his self-interest. Find ways he can be included in a larger social system with divergent people. At home, present theoretical and real moral dilemmas and explore various outcomes. Teach care reasoning skills.

Leadership

Leaders have a specific set of cognitive, social and technical skills, coupled with personality attributes. Leaders influence, assist and motivate others to achieve success. Leaders are designated the power figure behind a task or project either by appointment or through election and become the dominant figure in relationships at work or school and in community activities. Leaders manage their own and others activities in these settings without anxiety and with a high degree of self-confidence. In order to be a leader, you must have followers who agree to be led by you because they believe in your prowess or power. The leader defines the path to a goal, assigns people and material resources to achieve the goal, instructs people in how to accomplish their part of the project and manages the resources needed to complete the project.

More than just behavioral elements are required for a leader to be successful. People who have leadership as a core strength, exhibit leadership attributes such as power, authority, social assertiveness and charisma. They are confident and have vision, articulating what a successful outcome looks like and how to get there in easy to follow steps. Leaders are seen by their followers as loyal and without personal motive beyond success for the group. They are good organizers, cheerleaders and champions for the project.

You have evidence that leadership is a core strength because people are inspired when you take on a project and ask to work with you on the project. You have a knack for defining a problem, organizing people and resources to complete the project and getting it finished on time and on budget. You volunteer for complex projects and feel excited to take them on. When faced with a crisis or emergency you go on auto-pilot, take charge of the situation and you don't stop until the crisis is resolved. You enjoy inspiring others to do a better job and your followers often say "we couldn't have done it without you." You acknowledge the team that helped achieve the projects you are leading when you reach completion.

Your child has been assigned leaderships roles for several projects at school and none of them have gone as planned. Your child displays frustration about the failures and has now been assigned another opportunity to be a leader for a project. He becomes anxious and sullen. You have several choices. You can explain to him that he can graciously refuse to take on the leadership role but agree to participate as a follower to see if that is a more satisfying role for him. You can encourage him that practice makes perfect and that past failures do not insure future failures. You can enroll him in leadership training classes. You can tell him it is his social obligation to step up to the plate and do his duty. Or, you can ask him if he wants to be a leader or a follower and take his cue as to how to best support him, recognizing that not everyone wants to be or feels comfortable with taking on the responsibilities of leadership.

There are characteristics that inhibit one's abilities as a leader. People with a low propensity toward taking risks are less effective leaders. One study found that 40% of organizational change under new leadership was directly related to understanding the complexity of the work and being able to take risks. Exhibiting asocial behavior lessens the likelihood of finding enthusiastic followers. These asocial behaviors include secretiveness, hostility, disruptive behavior, lack of consideration for others, self-centeredness or not being sociable (relating to the group with warmth and inclusion.) People who are irritable, egocentric or dictatorial are not effective as leaders. If you or your child have these traits, leadership is not a core strength.

To teach children about leadership, parents must model the behaviors and attitudes of a leader. If leadership is not a parental core strength, but your child seems to behave like a leader, there is strong evidence that leadership training, primarily thorough self-help groups on leadership, is highly effective for both adults and children who have the temperament but not the skill set to effectively lead others. A child who is trustworthy, dynamic, communicative and makes plans and follows through to completion, may have the temperaments necessary for an effective leader.

Temperance – strengths that protect against excess

Forgiveness and Mercy

Those who access forgiveness and mercy as a signature strength recognize that forgiveness is an act of kindness not just to the transgressor but to themselves as well. When you forgive someone you become kinder and more generous, not just to the transgressor but to yourself as well. When you become less vengeful or avoidant, you become lighter and display a courageous vulnerability. People who have forgiveness and mercy as a core strength may be predisposed to forgiving as an overlying feature of their world view but forgiveness of a specific individual for a specific act may require considerable forgiveness work, even for the most adept forgiver.

Forgiveness does not excuse the other for their transgression or indicate you have forgotten what happened. Persons with the core strength of forgiveness may still choose to eject someone from their life even while forgiving them for the transgression. Forgiveness does not always include reconciliation. Reconciliation is where mercy plays a key role and how mercy distinguishes itself as a distinct process from forgiveness. People who have forgiveness as a core strength see genuine forgiveness as only taking place when completed with compassion, benevolence and love. They recognize as well that the transgressor doesn't necessarily deserve to be forgiven.

You have evidence that forgiveness and mercy is a core strength because you typically give people a second chance. You don't hold grudges and talk to people frankly about forgiving them for transgressions against you. You don't spend time thinking about how to get even. When you get angry with others, you quickly get past it and move on. You learn from betrayals and figure out how to frame a betrayal as a life lesson.

Children are not typically compassionate at a young age and forgiveness from a child, especially among his peers, may include an element of revenge (no mercy) before he is willing to forgive. Alternatively, the child may accept restitution over revenge for some transgressions. Regarding forgiveness, it has been shown that young children are least willing to forgive while seniors are more willing to forgive. Maturity allows for more forgiveness and as moral reasoning develops, people see forgiveness as a gift.

Your child tells his younger sibling that he cheated on an exam at school. She tells you that her sibling cheated and you confront him about it. He calls his sister a liar. You call her into the room and ask her, in front of him, if he told her he had cheated. She confirms this. You might say to him "While I forgive you for lying to me, you have broken two family rules. You know there are consequences for breaking rules so you will have two consequences." His sister might say "You called me a liar and I won't forgive you unless you let me use your computer for an hour tonight."

Multiple transgressions from a single person make it more difficult to forgive and even with apology, there is a diminishing return on apologizing if the transgressions follow a similar theme. You are less capable of forgiving, even if it is a core strength when you are angry, anxious, depressed or hostile. People with low empathy or perspective have more difficulty forgiving. Ruminating on the transgression interferes with the cognitive and emotional work necessary to forgive. Of the Big 5 personality traits, people who score high on neuroticism have difficulty forgiving or showing mercy.

Conversely, people who score high on the agreeableness scale of the Big 5 find it easier to complete a forgiveness process against their transgressors. Apologies promote forgiveness and perceiving that a transgression was unintentional rather than intentional makes it easier to forgive. Relationships that are close, have high satisfaction for the parties involved and have a commitment to continued success of the relationship prompt quicker forgiveness. Forgiving promotes mental and physical well-being and the result of genuine forgiveness improves positive emotions, thoughts and behaviors for both the transgressor and the forgiver. Genuine forgiveness reduces motivation for revenge or avoidance of the transgressor. To begin the forgiveness process, help your child (or yourself) learn to replace negative feelings with positive ones toward the transgressor, even if that person will no longer be a part of your life. Use empathy to understand why they may have betrayed you. Recognize you are giving them the gift of forgiveness even if they don't deserve it. Express gratitude that you have been able to transcend the hurt and pain as you begin to have better positive emotions as a result of the forgiveness. Dr. Robert Enright, a leading scholar on forgiveness, developed a 20 step model to learn to forgive. His premise is that a person must have been treated unjustly, decide to give up resentment about the unjust act(s) and offer goodness to the one who hurt you before you can truly forgive.

Self Control

People with a core strength of self-control regulate themselves well, are highly disciplined and control their emotions and desires. People exhibiting high levels of self-control use a process to ensure self-regulation. They set concrete goals. They conduct a comprehensive inventory to recognize discrepancies between where they are and where they want to be to determine the behaviors and attitudes that are interfering with the goal. They rigorously monitor their progress toward the goal. They are willing to stay the course, no matter what gets in the way. They consistently engage in behavior interruption from a response that would slow down progress.

Three types of control to remain mindful of, and distinguish between, are self-control, self-discipline and impulse control. Self-control is manifested when you have an urge to do something that is at variance to your moral values. Self-discipline is doing something you don't want to do. Impulse control is an intentional action counter to an irrational thought or potentially damaging behavior. People with good self-control are able to interrupt a behavior that will slow down the progress of reaching a desired goal. People with good self-control often self-administer punishments or rewards for getting off track or staying on track. Typically, these rewards and punishments are internalized but occasionally a reward or punishment is externalized.

     Your child enjoys playing the piano and has decided he will practice at least one hour every day. He rewards himself by purchasing new music to play every time he practices an hour a day, every day, for 2 weeks. He punishes himself if he misses a day by making up the time the next day and starting over with his two week count before rewarding himself with new music. Because he made the decision to set up this reward and punishment system, he is intrinsically motivated to become a more accomplished pianist with a by-product of increasing self-control. If you, as the parent, had set up this reward and punishment system, it would likely not be very effective in teaching self-control.

You have evidence that self-control is a core strength because when you put your mind to something, you always get the results you want. If you are diagnosed with Type II diabetes, you consult your health care provider, a diabetes educator and throw all the foods that are counter to your goal in the trash. You never veer from your exercise and diet routines. You only buy things when you can pay cash for them because you don't want to go into debt. You go to every one of your child's sports games, no matter what you would rather be doing. You don't smoke or drink even though you think about doing so nearly every day. You shop intentionally, knowing what you want to buy and avoiding going down aisles that you know don't have the products you intend to purchase.

Self-control is derailed for a variety of reasons. When we are under emotional stress or our energy is depleted, we give into self-indulgence over self-control. Simultaneous conflicting goals impair self-control. You attend a bridge club every Thursday. Your partner has tickets to the opera on a Thursday. Do you let your bridge partners down or do you let your partner down? Focusing on too many changes at once creates more diffused resolution and you may become depleted and lose self-control. Not paying attention to thought triggers that support control dysregulation can result in automatic behaviors and habits at variance to self-control. Indulgent parents who focus on immediate gratification and promote self-esteem over realistic feedback, like telling a child he did a good job when clearly he did not do a good job (because you don't want to damage self-esteem), do little to teach self-control to their child.

It is interesting to note that one study found that of thirty-two personality traits, the only one that could predict grade point averages was self-control. The literature does not report negative results for people who exercise a high level of self-control. To the contrary, children who exhibit high levels of self-control get better grades in school, are better at making personal adjustments in their life and make better relationship partners. One study followed four year olds who learned to delay gratification, a form of self-control. Ten years later, these children were more successful academically and socially than their peers.

The capacity to delay gratification may be set before the age of four for most people. Teach delayed gratification early in life by using the token system described in the Family Charter or other techniques you may prefer. Older children can be taught about delayed gratification through a variety of interventions. You may offer small rewards for an accomplishment now or a larger reward later. This only works if the child consistently sees the delayed reward as more valuable than the immediate reward and if the parent consistently follows through on delivering the larger reward. If the larger reward never comes, you are reinforcing immediate gratification and self-indulgence. To model impulse control, let your child help you make a list of items you will purchase at the grocery store each week. Buy nothing that is not on the list, even if it is a bargain or if you forgot to place an item on the list and will have to make a special trip to the store later. You can combine impulse control modeling with an exercise in delayed gratification by giving your child a choice of a small item now (like a piece of candy) or a larger item next week (like a box of cupcakes the whole family can enjoy together.)

Your child wants ice cream at the store and begins to have a tantrum when you say no. Indulgent parents give in because "I don't want him making a scene" or "it's just ice cream, why not let him have it" or "I'm just too tired to deal with this right now" or any other number of rationalizations. Show you child how to create a feedback loop to develop self-control. A feedback loop includes comparing the standard (what you want to accomplish) to behaviors that are oppositional to the standard, identifying what needs to change and how to behave differently. Finally, compare how the new behavior meets the standard. A feedback loop might include telling your child that if he wants ice cream he needs to put it on the grocery list before you go into the store or he will not get ice cream. If he starts to have a tantrum, he will be removed from the store and not be allowed to go to the store with you for one week.

Finally, teach your child to develop implementation intentions. Your child tells you she wants to lose five pounds before the homecoming dance. You agree this is realistic. You ask her how she intends to do that. Her implementation strategies include only eating salads at school and walking 20 minutes five times a week. Help her imagine she is succeeding at it and check in with her daily to see if she is on track. If not, use the feedback loop technique described above.

Humility

Of all the core strengths, humility is probably the least understood and least supported in American society. With an emphasis on self-esteem, families sometimes believe that teaching humility is the antithesis of developing good self-esteem in their children. To the contrary, humility is an important character strength. People with a core strength of humility are not afraid to admit their limitations, but they are able to also admit their successes. Humble people have an accurate view of their accomplishments and achievements. People with the core strength of humility do not seek the spotlight, but allow their achievements to speak for themselves, keeping those accomplishments in perspective and appreciating the value of other peoples' contribution to the success of a project. They don't see themselves as unique or special and exhibit a low focus on self. They are open to new ways of viewing things.

Humility is different from modesty although modesty may fall under the guise of humility. Modest people tend to be moderate in how they view their accomplishment, even to the point of denying their influence on an outcome. Modest people may express themselves to the outside world in low attention getting ways such as wearing modest clothing or having mannerisms that suggest they live a life of moderation. Modesty is a social virtue while humility is a character virtue. To borrow a quote from C.S. Lewis "Humility is not thinking less of yourself but thinking of yourself less."

You have evidence that humility is a core strength because you give credit where credit is due. You feel uncomfortable when someone overstates you contribution to the completion of a project and will assertively point out where you contributed and where you didn't. You are comfortable apologizing, when an apology is warranted. You become awestruck when contemplating natural wonders or the mysteries of the universe or a higher power.

You take your child on a trip through the desert. Because you live in a city, the light pollution obscures the majesty of the night time sky. Your family pulls to the side of the road so you can show your child the night time sky. As you lay across the hood of the car looking up into the sky, your child begins to softly cry. You ask what the problem is and your child replies "I never knew there could be so much beauty, I am overwhelmed. I am such a small speck of an enormous system."

Your child has many obstacles to overcome to learn about humility. In our society, in an effort to bolster self-esteem, some parents and educational institutions believe that unconditional praise, even when it is not an accurate accounting of an outcome, is a solution to good self-esteem. Gently leveling with your child teaches humility and gives him permission to understand his current limitations and gain better self-acceptance. It is generally accepted in this society that pride is a desired attribute. Pride gets in the way of humility. Acknowledging one's accomplishments is not boastful, bragging about them is. Permissive parenting, where parents are responsive but not demanding, may lead to a pleasant life for your child, but there is no evidence that it leads to a virtuous one. Humiliation and degradation of your child results in a loss of self-respect, dignity and pride in his accomplishments and may lead some to modesty behavior but not to humility.

How parents respond to the societal pressures of parenting makes an enormous difference in whether your child will learn about humility. You can model correction without defensiveness to your child to teach humility. Take responsibility for your mistakes or omissions and apologize when it is appropriate. Just the simple gestures of saying "I'm sorry" and "thank-you" goes a long way in teaching humility. Gratitude is often a generator of humility. You can model other-focused behavior over self-serving behavior in small day-to-day activities to reinforce humility. Other ways to teach your child about humility is to teach them self-acceptance and self-confidence. They do not, and in fact will not, excel in everything they try. Counter what they are not good at with what they are good at to help them love themselves and accept who they are. Remind you child that he develops mastery because of his effort not because he is better than others, smarter than others or more talented than others.

Prudence and Discretion

www.Wikipedia.com provides a trending site of the frequency that people research keywords in Wikipedia. On the topic of positive psychology, prudence is way down on the list compared to other signature strengths. Some people think that prudence is characterized by stinginess, thriftiness, self-sacrifice, self-restraint and excessive caution. The true characteristics of prudence include practical thinking, self-management, self-discipline and far-sightedness. People who have prudence as a core strength are future-minded individuals who tend to be conscientious, trustworthy and just. They act deliberately and resist impulses. Prudence is a person-oriented strength and prudent people tend to look at practical ways to achieve long term goals for self and family instead of having an other-centered orientation. Examples of prudence is saving for the future or planning for an unforeseen event. People who embrace prudence as a core strength are more physically fit, get better grades in school and have higher job and life satisfaction.

People with prudence as a core strength don't apply it to only one area of their lives but look at the whole life experience and determine a broad-based approach on how to harmonize all goals to improve overall well-being. Prudence requires discretion (making plans according to your own judgment about the right way to do things), discernment (acting wisely after examining all the alternatives) and discrimination (making fine distinctions about the best achievement process). People who have a core strength of prudence score higher on the Big 5 personality traits of agreeableness and extroversion.

You have evidence that prudence is a core strength because you live life joyfully and intentionally. You are a far sighted person who makes plans, takes reasoned risks and has successful outcomes. You stay on course with your long term goals because you planned well and are able to determine when you get off track. You have broad goals that cross all aspects of your life and you see the interconnectedness of each goal to the others. You are organized and systematic in taking on new goals. You don't walk alone on the street at night and you look both ways before crossing the street. You take risks, but you calculate the potential for harm or danger before taking those risks to eliminate the higher risk behaviors.

People are thwarted in their pursuit for prudence when they live in a highly chaotic environment. When carelessness goes unchallenged, children don't learn to be prudent. Acts of impulsivity are counter to prudence. Those who believe they have an uncertain future don't exercise prudence. Too much focus on a single goal and not paying attention to balancing priorities, leads to imprudence as does an emphasis on only setting short-term goals.

Your child is an avid swimmer and you support her swimming abilities. As an elementary school student, she exhibited characteristics of good problem solving, conscientiousness, delayed gratification, high socialization and self-confidence. Her coach says she is the best swimmer he has even seen in her age group. At swim meets across the state, you overhear from others that she has Olympic qualities. The entire family sacrifices resources to support her growth as a swimmer. Her grades begin to decline but you rationalize that she has a higher calling and accept her lack of attention to her studies. Throughout high school she wins most, but not all, of the swimming competitions. You continue to support her dream of competing at the Olympics. She has put friendships, academics and social interactions on the backburner and focuses all her attention on training. She gets a college scholarship for swimming but drops out of college her sophomore year because she believes school gets in the way of her training. She does not reach the finals for the Olympic Swim team and falls into a deep depressive episode. Was it prudent of you, and her, to forsake all the other well-being activities life has to offer to focus on a single outcome?

One study found that children who expressed high conscientiousness in middle school live longer than those who do not express this trait. Remember from the previous section that children express a capacity of deferred gratification around the age of four. Remember as well that prudence looks at the total life and doesn't put all the eggs in one basket. Teaching prudence is an important part of parenting. Simple modeling and interventions help your child understand prudence. Teach practical reasoning skills along with moral reasoning skills. Help your child reduce impulsivity by pointing out acts of impulsiveness and then determine alternative behavioral strategies. Help your child learn to set priorities across life domains to see how the goals interact and support or interfere with the whole life plan. Offer copious examples of discretionary caution by making observations such as "if you play in the street you have a greater risk of harm than if you play in the front yard at least ten feet from the street" or for adolescents contemplating sexual exploration or already engaged in sexual activity advising them to use a condom to reduce the risk of unwanted pregnancy or sexually disease transmission. For very young children, read stories to them about thoughtless action and the consequences of imprudence. Always help your child learn to be careful in their choices no matter what age they are. Using accurate memories about imprudent consequences, teaching open mindedness about alternatives and weighing pros and cons for each alternative path he can take, engaging in foresight and predicting the future based on each alternate path, applying caution but taking reasonable risk and reinforcing that balanced living is always the best course of action all reinforce the strength of prudence in your child's life.

Transcendence – strengths that connect us to the larger universe

Appreciation

Appreciation as a core strength enables one to see excellence and beauty in all things. Art, science, math, nature, skills, talents, and moral goodness all offer opportunity to experience appreciation. Those with the core strength of appreciation are able to experience moments of awe, admiration and elevation through everyday experience. They tend to seek out opportunity to increase positive emotions by paying attention to their surroundings. They find, recognize and take pleasure in goodness in both the physical and social world. Recognition of and response to beauty isn't just in the eye of the beholder. Appreciation of beauty is activated by the brain in the medial orbital frontal cortex (the pleasure center). Our perception of beauty of an object weakens as we begin to see flaws in the object. Aesthetic appreciation varies by individual and by culture. Westerners find more beauty in art that is symmetric while Eastern societies are drawn to asymmetrical art. However, when viewing faces perceived as beautiful, in all cultures the more symmetrical the face the more it is perceived as beautiful. Telling another that something is beautiful has little influence on the other's perception or appreciation of beauty. In the physical world, we know we perceive something as beautiful, and therefore good, through people, places, art and music. The response is one of awe. In the social world, we experience admiration for exceptional skills or talents of athletes, courageous people, artists and even politicians. We feel elevated when we see acts of moral goodness such as forgiveness or compassion. We feel bliss during a moving religious or spiritual experience. Awe, admiration, elevation and bliss are all transcendent states in that they reach beyond our cognitive world and reinforce that we are at home in the world and part of something greater than ourselves. Unlike the other strengths, there is no call to action associated with appreciation. Instead, we revel in the stillness of the experience. We are not searching for the utility of the object that stimulated the appreciation nor are we determining how to gain benefit from it beyond the positive emotion we experience.

You have evidence that appreciation is a core strength because you stop and smell the roses. You can't wait to get to the next exhibit at the museum. You scour the library for books of triumph against all odds. You go to hear a talk from an admired speaker. It's important to you that you surround yourself with things that are beautiful and you see beauty in all things.

Impediments to experiencing appreciation include the Big 5 personality trait of neuroticism. Not paying attention to your surroundings or what people are saying and doing that can inspire you reduces appreciation. People who are not open to new experience have less opportunity to find objects, people and ideas that can lead to appreciation. Likewise, people who exhibit low curiosity have fewer chances of finding elements to appreciate in their world. Those who experience chronic cynicism and pessimism afford themselves less ability to exercise appreciation.

While you can't teach your children to know what is beautiful, you can help them learn the emotional states that are associated with beauty and excellence. An appreciation of beauty begins with sensual beauty found in art, music, nature and people. As children age, appreciation becomes affixed not just to sensual beauty but to admiring skills and moral acts of courage. Help your child label their experiences of awe, admiration, elevation and bliss whenever they seem struck with recognizing appreciation. Appreciation almost always has an emotional and often tactile expression.

It is your child's first visit to the Botanical Gardens. She loves the wide variety of plants, pressing you on to each next display. Occasionally she stops to observe a plant. She is quieter than usual and takes in the surroundings with a big smile on her face. As you round a corner, there is a magnificent orchid in full bloom. She stops, takes a deep breath and a tear comes to her eye. She doesn't move and stares intently. You ask if there is a problem. She replies "No, this is just too amazing for words. I felt overwhelmed with joy and I got goose bumps when I saw this orchid. I just want to look at it for a while." What a great teaching moment for your child to learn how to experience and describe awe and an appreciation of beauty and excellence!

Gratitude

People with the core strength and disposition to gratitude know what they are thankful for and don't take the good things in life for granted. An expression of gratitude is thankfulness and joy derived from receiving a gift, both tangible (a present) and intangible (advice from someone you trust). Grateful people freely express appreciation of the gift and acknowledge that they understand the value of the gift. Gratefulness is two dimensional. Personal gratefulness is expressed to people who do something for you. Transpersonal gratitude is gratefulness to God or a higher power and is felt most strongly following a peak religious or spiritual experience. Gratitude expresses itself as a warm sense of appreciation and goodwill to the gift giver and is a call to action (saying thank you).

Several studies indicate that people who regularly access the core strength of gratitude have better physical health, less somatic complaints, higher optimism and positive states of alertness. They are more enthusiastic about life, more determined to reach goals and more attentive to others. They experience less depression and have higher life satisfaction. Grateful people are more likely to help others with a problem than people with a low disposition toward gratitude.

You have evidence that gratitude is a core strength because you frequently take the time to thank people when they have been kind or gone out of their way for you. You give generously and consistently to others. You have conviction that your life is easier because of the generosity others extend to you. You love Thanksgiving, because it honors the concept of gratitude. You reflect on the value of adverse events and recognize the gifts that come from them. You surround yourself with other grateful people and enjoy the opportunity to extend pro-social activities to them such as compassion, sympathy and emotional support.

Attributes of people with a low disposition to gratitude include selfishness, entitlement and preoccupation with materialism. They have a narrow perspective on life, often lack self-reflection skills and are chronic complainers. People who perceive themselves as passive or helpless victims show little gratitude in their overall life. People who fail to access the strength of gratitude often believe there is a smaller group of people to thank than those who have gratitude as a core strength.

Over dinner, you share the good news that you were just promoted. You use yourself as an example of how hard work and persistence pays off. You brag a little about how you set yourself up for the promotion and pushed out the competition. You tell them you were in the right place at the right time and that when you overheard a conversation that this position was coming available you began a campaign to show off your skills. Your teenager asks you if you are thankful to anyone about getting the promotion and you say you are grateful the hiring manager had the good sense to pick you. She reminds you that you should also be grateful to those who taught you the skills to prepare you for this position, your old boss who certainly influenced the decision, your co-workers who helped you finish past projects and even your teachers in school.

Research indicates that people raised in the United States are less comfortable with personal gratitude conceptually than persons raised in Asian cultures. Persons in the United States express personal gratitude less frequently than most cultures. Finally persons with high narcissism report that the experience of gratitude is unpleasant and the expression of gratitude appears more manipulative than sincere.

Most barriers to increasing gratitude can be changed through cognitive and behavioral modification. It is important to note that the literature reports that children under the age of six do not benefit from the strength of gratitude. They may say thank you on cue ("That nice person gave you a piece of candy, what do you say?") but it is not a spontaneous act driven by the strength of gratefulness, merely a demonstration of politeness. Between the ages of seven to ten, a child begins to grasp the concept of gratitude. None the less, you can help your child learn about the concept even at a very young age by telling age appropriates stories about the gifts that life has to offer. There is evidence that a child learns about gratitude not through the use of politeness skills but by hearing stories and participating in activities that show how the community benefits from gratitude in action. The most powerful way to build and broaden gratitude awareness, and the positive emotions that come about through the expression of gratitude, is through the use of a gratitude journal. The positive outcomes described in the beginning of this section were measured by the use of gratitude journals. People wrote down a list of what they were grateful for each day for a specified period of time. Other groups either wrote down neutral events of the day or negative events of the day, depending on the study. Through pre-test and post-test results and longitudinal follow-up, there were distinct differences between the group that expressed gratitude, via journal entry, and those who did not keep a gratitude journal. Once you and your child practice this daily for a few weeks, you can begin to automatically recount what you are grateful for in your head each night before you go to bed.

Hope

People with the core strength of hope consistently expect the best in the future and are willing to work to accomplish it. They believe the future is in their control and they are the masters of their destiny. Hope supports achievement. Without hope, people do not move toward their goals. People with the core strength of hope are optimistic, invest the necessary time, financial and emotional resources into the possibilities that lie in the future for them and believe that they influence the outcomes of their goals. They further believe that good events increase over time and bad events decrease over time based on the actions they take.

Three models of hope and the likelihood of being optimistic (hopeful) or pessimistic (hopeless) have been the subject of research studies. Dr. Charles Carver and Dr. Michael Scheier (the researches that created the feedback loop model described in the strength of self-control earlier) posit a self-regulatory model to extend hope. The self-regulation model proposes that good things are plentiful and bad things are scarce. Dr. Charles Snyder's Hope Theory describes two ingredients necessary for hope - agency and pathway - with agency (the agent) being determination and pathway being direction (the course you take). Dr. Martin Seligman uses an explanatory style (how you explain good and bad events in your life) to increase hope and optimism. See the section How to Foster a Flourishing Family to review explanatory styles.

You have evidence that hope is a core strength because, despite your present challenges, you are convinced things will get better for you. You look on the bright side of things, finding the good in every situation. You garden, knowing that gardeners always look for future growth. You strongly believe that you can reach the goals you set for yourself. You plan for the future and have a five year, ten year and twenty year plan you are working toward. You never go into a competition thinking you might lose.

You help someone who is down in the dumps by expressing hope for the future and reminding her that things keep improving.

There is some evidence that socioeconomic status impacts hope but it is not conclusive. One study found that lower class youth in the United States are present minded, a condition that is oppositional to hope and optimism, and that upper class youth are future oriented. Since optimism can be learned, this is of small consideration in developing hope as a core strength. The greater obstacles to overcome are lack of future mindedness, pessimism and learned helplessness.

Your child loves being in the water and is especially fond of diving. He has a fear of heights so he limits himself to the low board. When he comes to you and says he wants to join the diving team, you remind him that he likely will be expected to compete in both low board and high board events. He tells you he is ready to conquer his fear of heights and you offer to go to the pool with him to offer support and encouragement. He climbs halfway up the ladder, freezes for a moment, and climbs back down the ladder. With tears in his eyes, he tells you he has to give up his dream of becoming a competitive diver. You offer him hope for the future by telling him that there are scientifically proven ways for him to overcome his fear of heights and not to give up just yet. You explain the technique to him and ask if he has any questions. You ask whether he wants your help or if he wants your help in finding a professional to help him. He asks for your help first and says if that doesn't work, he always has a second chance with the professional (his expression of hope). Together you construct an exposure hierarchy (See the section How to Foster a Flourishing Family to review the technique) and move step-by-step through the process. You take him back to the pool. He climbs the stairs and dives off the high board without hesitation. You congratulate him and he says "thanks, now it's time for me to get to work if I'm going to win any medals."

Hope seems to develop naturally in a child unless there is an interfering factor such as absence of attachment. Children around the age of eight can be taught about explanatory styles and this leads to more optimism. Snyder believed that the two ingredients in Hope Theory (determination and direction) are sequentially developed in children with direction being acquired before determination. It has also been reported in the literature that active participation in an orthodox religion builds hope in youth and adults. Another deliberate intervention to build hope and optimism as a core strength is educating your school on the importance of including assignments of hopeful narratives. Since children don't developmentally understand optimism until after they enter school, school is an important contributor to building optimism. Assign your child reading that instills hope and optimism. Give them instructions on setting goals and how to achieve them to help them become future-oriented. Monitor their optimism and point out when optimism bias can lead to imprudent action.

Spirituality

Spirituality is a conviction that there is a non-physical dimension to life, a power that is higher than human beings, that is sacred and divine. It is that higher power which guides one's life. For those with a core strength of spirituality, the conviction is pervasive and stable. Dr. Sigmund Freud believed that God is an illusion invented by people so they could look up to a father figure that would unconditionally love and protect them as no human father could. People of faith do not agree.

While the words spiritual and religious are often used interchangeably, in this section they have a slightly different connotation. Religious is used to describe the public practice of your beliefs in God or a higher power (the divine) through adherence to the beliefs and rituals that glorify the divine one. Spiritual is used in this discussion when referring to the private relationship between you and the divine and the virtues that lead to a life of goodness as a result of that relationship.

There is significant evidence that religion develops and maintains values that support the social order in a culture. No culture is without the belief of the divine. The benefits of religious affiliation and spiritual practice are well documented. Faith in a higher power satisfies emotional needs, stabilizes one's life and gives one the opportunity to express gratitude through worship and service.

You have evidence that spirituality and religion is a core strength because you have a deep and abiding faith in the divine. You and your family regularly attend services. Your values and morals are aligned to the teachings of a higher power. You pray. Your beliefs give you comfort in times of illness and need. You live your life righteously.

> Your child comes to you with a moral dilemma. You and he sit down with the sacred text of your faith to find passages that will guide his decision. You pray together about it and he has a strong sense of knowing what path to take, based on living a life with purpose, according to his beliefs and with divine guidance.

Over their counterparts, youth active in religion avoid antisocial activity, have lower rates of alcohol and drug experimentation and greater emotional self-regulation. They are less aggressive, have better academic performance, delay sex longer and see the world as more comprehensible. When they are with peers who are also religious, they express greater empathy toward one another and are less antagonistic. Religious parents have lower levels of marital conflict, more consistent parenting and more supportive relationships with each other and with their children.

Parents have a strong influence over their children's religious socialization. While mothers seem to have greater control of the religious institutional affiliation (are more likely to choose the church, synagogue or mosque), there is evidence to support that fathers strongly influence their sons' beliefs and religious involvement (sons go to church at the same frequency as their dads) but mothers influence the ways sons apply religious values in everyday life.

It has been found that a child raised in a nuclear family where the mother is not working outside the home full-time and where both parents have similar beliefs, spiritual practices and religious involvement has a greater likelihood to retain religious involvement into adulthood. Families who attend more orthodox institutions have less depression, greater well-being and better overall physical health than families who attend more liberal institutions. It is also reported that social networks promote or diminish spiritual and religious development.

Humor

Humor, in the transcendent sense, is not well studied. It is a core strength in the sense that it lifts us outside of ourselves and produces positive emotions and well-being. Humor is linked to good mood and mitigates bad mood by taking the edge off of threatening situations. Humor is related to playfulness and people with a core strength of humor also exhibit a lot of playfulness. Humor is, after all, playing with ideas. Nonsense humor is the humor that children learn about, primarily through doing silly things, being ridiculous and memorizing jokes and riddles. Nonsense humor does little to comfort self or others or build positive emotions, but it is good for a quick laugh. Nonsense humor decreases after age sixteen. Incongruity-resolution humor, the humor that understands the vagaries of life but tolerates and forgives them because life is never perfect, increases with age and life experience.

You have evidence that humor is a core strength because when your friends are down, you reach into your humor bag to cheer them up. You approach all your tasks playfully and get pleasure out of elevating others with your playfulness. You are always able to find something funny to comment on, no matter how dire the situation. You frequently laugh heartily and with sincerity about life's ups and downs. People say you are fun to be with, the life of the party.

Overemphasis on being serious impedes playfulness. Not all cultures appreciate external expressions of playfulness but humor is universal. One study found that mothers of class clowns are less kind, less sympathetic, less close to their child, more selfish and more controlling. Their children appear to learn about nonsense humor as a method to gain approval from peers and exhibit their goodness to others.

The ability to create humor is linked to intelligence and creativity and the literature indicates that a humorous attitude about life is the product of a cheerful temperament. There is little scientific evidence that humor can be cultivated. Indeed some humor is destructive and you don't want to cultivate that in you or your child. Satire, cynicism, sarcasm and mockery gets laughs but at the expense of another. Humor's highest good as a core strength is breaking tension with a sympathetic heart and finding humor in every day disappointments.

Your six year old child is experiencing his first family funeral and observes how sad and somber everyone is during the memorial service. When family and friends gather at the home after the burial, he notices that things are lightening up and hears a group of people laughing. He goes over to this group, thinking they are telling jokes. What he discovers is that they are recalling amusing stories about the deceased to comfort each other in their grief. He doesn't understand what is happening. This is one of those rare legitimate times you can say to him "You are too young to understand, but you will understand what happened today when you get older. For now, just know that older people use humor to help others not feel so sad."

Bringing it together

Identifying your child's core strengths is the first step to increasing well-being and emotional health. Using those strengths builds resiliency and inoculates against depression and anxiety. Research estimates that 15-20% of children will experience an episode with depression by the end of high school, one in eleven will experience an episode of depression by the end of middle school and that 75-80% of those students will not receive treatment for depression. Dr. Jane Gillham and Dr. Karen Reivich directed a program called The Penn Resiliency Project where fifth and six graders at risk for depression were exposed to a twelve week class that taught problem solving and coping strategies. To see a presentation of their findings, remarkable indeed, go to http://www.ppc.sas.upenn.edu/gillhampowerpoint.pdf . A total of thirteen studies with over 2000 participants had completed this intervention by 2007.

The following is a cross walk presented by Gillham and Reivich for which character strengths are bolstered by the problem solving module of this intervention.

Emotional awareness training

Social/Emotional Intelligence

Perspective

Assertiveness and Negotiation

Social/Emotional Intelligence

Intimacy (Love and being loved)

Fairness

Bravery

Team work

    Self-control

    Kindness

    Integrity

Examining alternatives

    Social/Emotional Intelligence

    Perspective

    Self-control

    Judgment

Problem solving and decision making

    Judgment

    Persistence

    Bravery

    Prudence

    Creativity

    Hope

Self-control

Find activities, assignments, tasks and chores where you and your child can use your core strengths. The strengths you share can be used as a family but each of you have core strengths different from the remainder of the family. Honoring those strengths, especially if they are in the bottom of your strength list can be challenging. The next section of this book will show you how to create a Family Charter. Now that you have identified the strengths of each member of your family, look at rewards and chores that align with each family member's core strength.

Remember that the reason you build and broaden core strengths is to increase positive emotions, build resiliency and improve family well-being. Don't focus on the liabilities but rather on the assets to get best results. Nevertheless, results on VIA may change over time as you pay attention to and exercise your latent character strengths.

The Family Charter

The Family Charter

What is a Family Charter?

A Family Charter is the roadmap to greater harmony and cooperation in your household. It is a systematic approach to helping your children learn about responsibility, justice, temperance, kindness, gratitude, hope and wisdom. The system is effective because each family member knows just how she or he can contribute to the family, what to expect if they break a family rule, how to obtain rewards and privileges and how to regain a stronger footing toward the future.

It works for children because it offers guidance and a clear understanding of what is expected of them. It works for parents because they are able to refer back to the charter when a child breaks a rule or asks for a reward. It is a fair system that is evenly and consistently applied, without exception. Everyone in the family knows what to expect and how to live in a loving and flourishing family.

The basic blueprint for constructing the Family Charter is to generate a Family Mission Statement, define household rules clearly, establish realistic consequences that are consistent and give children a way to be rewarded for their achievements and receive immediate feedback when they have violated the Family Charter.

Most important of all, a Family Charter releases parents from being "the bad guy" or the punisher. Children learn to take full responsibility for their actions. Consequences, either positive or negative, reinforce a more virtuous life. The next section will explain the five part system which includes

- Mission Statement
- Rules
- Consequences
- Rewards
- Chores

How to write a mission statement

A mission statement is a brief summary of what your family believes in. When thinking about your family's mission statement, begin at the end and work backwards. What do you want to accomplish as parents? What is important for your child's success as a virtuous adult? Write a family mission statement as if you were writing a mission statement for your business based on the correct principles for your family. Think about why your family exists and what its core purpose is. What do you want to be remembered for after your children have grown up?

Mission statements are short, do not have more than four of five objectives and inspire the family to be forward thinking. A mission statement drives the behaviors of your family. Avoid creating a flowery, fluffy or wordy statement no one will be inspired by or remember. A good rule of thumb is to determine the answers to two questions. How do we want our family to operate? How do we propose to do it?

The family mission is something the whole family can create together in families with older children. A sample Family Mission Statement follows.

The Waldring Family Charter Mission Statement

"The Waldring Family is a loving and supportive family that strives to always be respectful, safe and cheerful. It is our mission to treat everyone fairly, to disagree respectfully and to honor the feelings of others. We are a family with clear values and purposeful rules. We co-operate in maintaining a clean and honest household. In this household our goal is to raise productive, loving successful adults."

Family Rules

Many families are looking for a quick-fix checklist of family rules. Unfortunately, there is no "one size fits all" when it comes to developing the rules section of your family charter. Customs, values, time available to spend with family, age of children, possible co-parenting challenges such as children living in two households, and a host of other considerations must be woven into a Family Charter. The best way to begin to develop a rules section of your personal Family Charter is to break down into subsets how you want your family to operate.

Some essential areas to address include:

- Family attitude about remaining lawful (including parental curfews)

- Family attitude about intrafamily respect, loyalty, integrity, honesty

- Family attitude about community and social life

- Family attitude about school and work life

- Family attitude about household maintenance

- Family attitude about spiritual or religious activities

- Family attitude about health such as exercise, diet, emotional health

- Other important family attitudes

After determining the broadly defined categories that are important in your household, begin to brainstorm the rules associated with each category. Remember to pick your battles wisely. Most rules sections have no more than 50 household rules and a few rules may be different for different age groups. Most rules however are true for any age group. Whether a child is 2, 12 or 22, a parent should never allow a child to physically or verbally abuse them without a consequence.

An important caveat for parents is that unless you are prepared to deliver a consequence each time the rule is broken, it does not belong on your list. Once you have published your rules and consequences list, it becomes non-negotiable. If anyone feels the list needs modification, it is to be suggested at a family meeting. However, the rule is best left on the books until the next family meeting when parents will either inform the family the rule is eliminated or that it will be continued and whether the consequence will remain the same or be changed. The same is true for any new rule that will be placed on the list. It will be suggested at one family meeting and then ratified, modified or revoked at the next family meeting as a two-step approach.

While it might appear too cumbersome to use a two-step approach when changing, adding or eliminating a rule or consequence in the Family Charter, nothing could be further from the truth. Violating the two step process dilutes the strength of the charter for the parent because children won't take the system seriously. Children will learn they can manipulate the charter and you will quickly find your charter expands and contracts every month. Remember that the purpose of a Family Charter is to teach consistency and reliability for both parent and child. A solid Family Charter should be a living document based on the changing needs of the family circumstances. Examples include changing the time a child goes to bed or curfew times as children get older, adding a rule about driving privileges when a child gets a driver's license or how many times a child can participate in sleepovers in a month.

The following section offers several examples of possible rules within each category listed above. It is merely illustrative. Only you, as parents, can know what rules are really important in your household based on your attitudes, values and norms.

Family rules about remaining lawful (including parental curfews)

1. Federal state and local laws shall be followed at all times

2. Alcohol, drugs, tobacco and all other items that are illegal for a minor to possess will never be in your possession (even if you are holding them for a friend)

3. Obey authority at home, work, school and in the community. If you think you have been treated unfairly, talk with us about it when you get home. The only exception is if you have been abducted or someone is attempting to abuse you (you will be expected to file a police report.)

4. You will be home at the declared curfew time. You may call us within 15 minutes of curfew time if you are going to be late to reduce the consequences when you arrive home late. For every minute you are home later than the agreed upon time, your consequences will become greater.

5. You may not harm yourself, other people or animals.

Family rules about intrafamily respect, loyalty, integrity, honesty

1. No hitting, screaming, pushing, threatening or verbally abusive behavior is allowed in the home.

2. Every family member will attend family meetings ON TIME and behave respectfully during the meeting (no groans, acting foolish, leaving "in a huff" or pouting). You may express your concern respectfully about a discussion if you have an alternative to explore.

3. When you are assigned character cards, you will take them without complaint or acting out and complete them timely.

4. When a parent says no, it means no. You may not continue to ask without consequences.

5. Borrowing something that is not yours without permission is prohibited. This includes the reading of any personal diaries without permission. This family considers such acts of borrowing without permission to be theft. Since

you are expected to remain lawful, an infraction will result in two consequences.

Family rules about community and social life

1. You will attend scheduled family outings in as cheerful a manner as is appropriate to the occasion.

2. If you do not wish to attend a family outing, you must state it when it is first suggested along with a specific reason why you do not think this outing will build positive experience and memory for the family. However, it is still the parents' decision about whether you are expected to attend.

3. You will remain co-operative and respectful when there are guests in your home or when you are a guest at another's home or office.

4. You must have permission to go anywhere and stay only where you have been given permission to go. If you want to go to additional places beyond your original destination, you will call us to ask permission.

5. If you break rules and your friends are visiting or scheduled for a visit, you have lost your privilege to entertain. Your friends' parents will be informed of this rule and condition. You will not continue to interact with your friend even if he or she remains in the house until a prearranged pick-up time.

Family rules about school and work life

1. You will bring your homework home each day, complete it on time and show the competed homework to your parent or a designated person who can check it.

2. You will not break rules, including bus rules, and will remain respectful and co-operative with teachers and fellow students.

3. If you get in a fight (verbal or physical) at school you will be given consequences. It does not matter who started the fight.

4. If you have a job, you are responsible for maintaining it. Although we may assist you in getting to and from work, it is your obligation

to find alternative transportation, if necessary. As parents, we will not intervene in the employer/employee relationship unless we believe you are in danger. Working is a privilege, not a right, and you may only work if you maintain your school grades and follow household rules.

5. If you know you are doing poorly in a subject, you will inform us as soon as you become aware you are falling behind. As parents, we will arrange for tutoring or additional work to help you catch up. Failure to tell parents timely about deficiencies at school will result in a consequence.

Family rules about household maintenance

1. Everyone in the household will participate in household maintenance. You must complete your daily and weekly chores to parental satisfaction on time and without complaint. As parents, we want you to succeed; therefore we will show you what "satisfactory" means to us up to two times without complaint.

Beyond that, "unsatisfactory" will result in consequences.

2. You may not "trade" chores with another without parental permission.

3. Dishes and food may not be left in common areas such as the living room or in your room. All dirty dishes and food must be put up before bedtime.

4. You may not play music, television or other devices at a volume that is disturbing to others. If you are asked to turn down volume, and fail to do so, the device will be turned off.

5. Do not blame another for a mess if you are asked to clean it up. The purpose of the request is not to affix blame but to fix a problem that makes the household run less efficiently.

Family rules about spiritual or religious activities

1. You will be respectful and attentive at religious functions.

2. You will participate in spiritual or religious activities at home such as prayer, meditation or devotional or philosophic activities.

3. You sit with the family at religious or social functions unless parents suggest otherwise.

4. No swearing or talking about inappropriate subject matter.

5. You will abide by the moral code agreed upon in your household. This includes demonstrating wisdom, courage, love, justice, temperance, forgiveness and appreciation.

Family rules about health such as exercise, diet, emotional health

1. You will not eat foods that have been declared off-limits. You will eat sufficient food to nourish the body every day.

2. You will spend some time each day in outdoor physical activity (weather permitting) or indoor physical activity, of at least 30 minutes a day at least 5 days a week.

3. You will take, without being reminded (if old enough), all medications and perform all physical therapy exercises (if given.)

4. You will talk about feelings to us. It's OK to talk about being angry in a calm and rational way. If you talk about being angry with one of us to the other of us, you will not keep it a secret, even if you are no longer angry. You do not have to share the content of the conversation, simply inform us both that you are working through a feeling of anger. We are here to listen to your anger but you should not expect us to "fix" what made you angry. When you express your anger you will use the following sentence map:

    I feel angry because _____ and I want or need _____.

    Consequences for expressing anger or disappointment will never be given as long as you use this sentence map and speak calmly and respectfully.

Other important family rules

1. Do not play with lighters or matches. Do not burn candles or incense without parental approval and adult supervision.

2. Parents' room is off limits without specific permission to enter. No eavesdropping on private conversations between parents.

3. Attend all scheduled appointments on time, without complaining.

4. Family meals are to be a shared cheerful experience for all family members with discussions about what positive events happened today. Serious or potentially disturbing discussions with us are to be completed at least 15 minutes before dinner or started at least 15 minutes after dinner, never during dinner.

5. Continued refusal to co-operate with family rules may lead to the consequence of removal from the household and placement in a boarding school or long term residential treatment facility in a location that may be far away from the family. As parents, we will do everything we possibly can to keep our family together under the same roof. If residential treatment/intervention is necessary, we will not

hesitate to act. If as parents, we feel we need to exercise this option for your own safety, or the safety of our family, we will give you a specific set of rules that lets you know what you must do to remain in the home. In the event you must live in a residential facility away from home, you will be gone a minimum of thirty days to nine months and possibly longer. As parents, we commit to follow the recommendations of the treatment facility regarding visitation and other guardianship issues.

While the above lists are actual family rules that come from Family Charters I have helped families work on, few may fit your family. These examples are included to help you think about what is really important in your household and illustrate how they may be worded. Note that although these rules may use the word consequence, they do not typically list what the consequences are. The next section will help you explore how to set consequences and publish them for each family member to refer to.

Consequences

Remembering that there is a difference between punishment and consequences, this section is devoted to ideas related to character building consequences rather than punishments. Taking things away from a child or verbally abusing or physically disciplining or humiliating a child does little to create more than a compliant/defiant relationship. That is to say the child either says "I'll do what I have to do to get by without being punished" or "I don't care how you punish me, I'm not going to comply and you can't make me!" Evidence shows that adding consequences is much more effective than punishments for several reasons. First consequences are named in advance so there are no surprises as with punishment, which tends to happen "on the fly" and is often inconsistent. Punishment has a separate objective from consequences but punishment can remain a part of your overall parenting style.

Have you ever heard someone say "If you talk back, you're gonna' get a whack." When a child is told this, he learns how to have opinions but not talk about them. It does little more than make the child fearful to talk about ideas because it could be wrongly interpreted as "back talk". A better defined rule is "if you disagree with me and do so respectfully, that is not talking back. However, if you are rude, say cruel things or raise your voice when you disagree with me, that is talking back and there will be a consequence for your <u>lack of respect</u>, not because you have an opinion."

Children who are encouraged to express a differing opinion extends a character building activity for your child, helps reinforce their assertiveness skills and also gives a parent insight into how your child views the world. When a child is given permission to disagree, and to explain why he disagrees, the parent simply rolls with the resistance. It will likely not change your mind, but the child has just had a demonstration of fairness and justice. A sentence map parents might adopt could be "I understand that you _____ (paraphrase the objection of the child), however _____ (give your reasons for rejecting his opposition) so I intend to remain firm in my decision." If you won't accept your child's counter suggestion, using this phrase consistently will quickly break your child from any "but…" responses.

Consequences can be both additive and subtractive. Additive consequences include additional chores, responsibilities and activities whereas subtractive consequences include taking away privileges, physical items or time with family. The most effective consequences are immediate, achievable and for a specific time.

The phrase "grounded for life" is not a consequence at all and most parents are really not prepared to refuse to allow a child to have any social activity for an extended period of time.

Consequently, being grounded loses meaning for the child and becomes a "waiting game" to see how long it will be before the parent gives in. When a parent says, "you are grounded for a month", only to begin to make exceptions (the homecoming dance, a call from the child's best friend on the child's birthday, an opportunity to try out for a school play, a visit to the zoo because the rest of the family had planned for it), grounded is not grounded anymore. Many children learn about "being grounded" from a very young age. For toddlers and preschoolers, it's called time-out. Time out is a consequence that is effective, based on a child's understanding of time-out being related to a singular behavior, for up to about a minute per year of age. Time-outs of longer duration have little added effect.

In this book, consequences and chores have very different meanings. Chores are household responsibilities that build mastery, help children feel like valuable, contributing members of the household, teach teamwork and increase problem solving. Additive consequences are extra chores or activities and are not directly related to household maintenance. For example a consequence of going to a friend's house without permission might be to scrub the bathtubs, even if another had just thoroughly cleaned the bathroom two hours earlier.

Random infractions of a rule require certain randomness to the consequence to remain effective. That is to say, when a child occasionally breaks a rule there is always a consequence but that consequence may be a number of different activities. You want to come up with a list of at least 50 possible consequences. Dr. Matthew Johnson described a technique from behavioral psychology in his book Family RULES where he asks parents to create a deck of good habit cards, each with a consequence written on it. Based on the severity of the rule broken, a family member must draw a certain, pre-assigned number of cards and complete the tasks on those cards before the rule violation has been wiped away. Some consequence ideas follow but this is only a starting point. You will need to find age appropriate consequence activities that work for your family.

- Wash four interior windows.
- Remove all shirts from their closet and replace them based on darkest to lightest color.
- Wash the car or vacuum the interior.
- Do fifty jumping jacks or jump rope for five minutes.
- Scrub all toilets and tubs in the house.
- Wash and fold all towels (even the clean ones).

- Wash all wastepaper baskets in the tub, and then clean the tub.

- Read an article on the subject of parent or sibling choice and write a 300 word report about it.

- Write a letter explaining why breaking the rule was more important than any consequence in the deck.

- Write 100 times, "When I break a rule, I have consequences."

The above list was additive and these tasks can be accomplished fairly quickly, within a matter of minutes in some cases. Note that the consequences have varying degrees of time investment, labor and complexity. Further, none of the examples are routine household maintenance chores. Additionally, this deck of consequences cards, which I like to call Character Cards, are random and the person doesn't know what the consequence will be until the card is drawn from the deck. It bears repeating that everyone knows in advance what the rules are and have chosen to take the chance of getting any of these consequences for breaking the rules. Now let's turn our attention to subtractive consequences.

- No visits or telephone calls from friends for 3 days

- Television, stereo, electronic games and computer will remain turned off for 24 hours.

- Reading material will be taken from your room and you may only read textbooks from school

- You may not engage in "family fun time" for the next 24 hours

- You will eat dinner alone tonight (or tomorrow night)

- You may not enter the family room for 24 hours

Add a couple cards in to breakdown resistance to using the Character cards and to help build experience around hope and mercy such as

- "Lucky break – this card is blank",

- assign one chore to the parent or sibling of your choice

- This card entitles you to negotiate a time for 15 uninterrupted minutes with a parent doing whatever you want to do that is creative and fun without interruption or interference from other family members.

Often parents tell me they are worried that their children will not do the tasks they draw. As a parent, the best way to get your family started on the assigned task from the Character Card is to refuse to interact about anything else until the tasks are completed. No matter what, refuse to interact about anything else. It will only take a few times for your child to get the message you mean business and then things will get considerably more cheerful and cooperative in the house. For example, your child says, "I'm not going to do that and you can't make me. " Your response is, in a calm and matter-of-fact tone, "You are right I can't and I won't try to make you do it. However, we have nothing further to discuss until you satisfactorily complete the task." Your child may go stomping off to her room (which adds some more Character Cards to her already growing list of consequences.) Ignore her entirely.

When it is mealtime, go to her room and ask if the consequences have been completed. If not, take her meal to her room and inform her, in a loving voice, you are sad she has chosen not to eat with the family. Twenty minutes later, go back to her room to get the dishes and simply announce, "I am here to clear your dishes" and say nothing more. When she attempts to interact later that evening, you gently remind her "I'd love to talk to you about that, but I can't until you complete your task cards. You have a few more consequences as well as the ones you already have since you were disrespectful, stomped off to your room and refused to accept consequences. When you complete the first set, you can draw the remaining Character Cards from the deck."

Remember, no matter what, answer no questions, give no permission for any activity and refuse to argue. Become a broken record. "I'm sorry but everything is on hold until you complete your consequences." Remain solidly frozen on your task until she chooses to satisfactorily complete the Character Cards. You can anticipate needs, like lunch money, and give it to her. If she asks for anything that will not directly negatively influence her schoolwork or health, refuse to discuss it with her until the tasks are completed. Once all Character Cards are satisfactorily completed, simply say thank you and don't bring up any of what you have had to endure. Instead, act as if it was effortless for you to tolerate her outrageous and defiant behavior. Then resume the relationship, letting her talk about anything. If you have to repeat this process more than three times, email me at daniel@howfamiliesflourish.com and we can figure out how sabotage is taking place.

Rewards

Exactly what are rewards? Some parents think of a reward as a large item of great monetary value given on very special events. A glamorous wedding, a senior trip to Europe, a "sweet sixteen" bash with live band, a thirteenth birthday party to mark the teen years, a computer to commemorate entering school. These might more be categorized as treasures than rewards. A reward is anything earned and represents, in a physical way, a challenge that was met. Some parents confuse reward with privilege, although rewards and privileges are more interchangeable than rewards and treasures.

A privilege is getting to try out for t-ball, taking karate lessons, an ice cream cone at your child's favorite ice cream shop, a shopping excursion, being able to attend or host a sleep-over, going to a school dance, dating, getting to drive the car. A privilege is something you allow your children to do because they have successfully completed other things. For example, no matter how pleased you are your son has made the varsity football team, and no matter how talented he may be at football, your son is not entitled to be on the team. It is a privilege afforded him by the school only if he maintains a certain conduct and academic discipline. Hopefully, if your child were failing at school, missing classes and picking fights with other students, you would recognize that the privilege of playing on the team should be suspended or revoked.

Why would it be different at home? If you child breaks rules, picks fights and refuses to participate in the family, your child can build character by learning that "privileged activity" can and will be withheld until there is a behavior and attitude change. Even if your child is about to qualify for black belt status, if she is using those skills to beat up her irritating little brother, her privilege to continue should be suspended or revoked. This may sound like an extreme case so let's reduce it to everyday family life.

Your child wants a new toy. Is your child entitled to it? Absolutely not. Can your child earn it as a reward? Absolutely. But how do you determine and your child become aware when she has done enough to earn the reward of that desired toy? You introduce a token economy into your reward system. Token economies have been used for many years and are a foundational pillar of behavioral psychology. Reward behaviors that are desired; ignore behaviors that are not. Dr. B.F. Skinner demonstrated this when he developed what has been nicknamed the "Skinner box". Its fancy name is operant conditioning chamber. If you took a psychology course in high school or college you may have placed a laboratory rat in one of these chambers, filled a tube with food and then recorded how many times it took for the animal to learn that when he stepped on a bar, a food pellet dropped down. Eventually the rat learned that when he pressed the bar, he obtained a food pellet, or a reward. Based on the idea of operant conditioning, Dr. Ted Allyon and some of his colleagues began using a reward system to shape desired behavior with institutionalized people. After these patients collected enough tokens, or "gold stars," they could go to a campus store and turn them in for personal items, food or other things. The more tokens, the larger the reward.

You can adapt this technique quite easily in your household. Obtain poker chips of various colors so each child has his or her own color to avoid confusion. Remember that rewards (and tokens represent a way to build toward a meaningful reward) are given because a certain behavior occurred and, once earned, are not taken away. Therefore, tokens being taken away from a family member should NEVER be on your consequence list.

An easy way to introduce a token reward system is to offer one token per day that all chores have been completed satisfactorily, without parental prompting and without complaint from your child. Some families add a bonus if all chores are completed as above for an entire week. A second way your child can earn tokens is by you identifying a rule that is often broken (such as talking back despite the consequence) and giving a set number of tokens for every week there was no rule violation. If he breaks no rules for four weeks he could earn an additional bonus. If you have more than one child in the household, they should get an equivalent number of tokens for weekly and four week full compliance with the rules of the household to keep things fair. You will be surprised how motivating a token economy is!

Yet another way for children to earn tokens is through demonstrations of their personal strengths. You might want to offer a small reward for each time you observe them using a strength with mastery and a predetermined number of these small tokens could be cashed in for the larger token (for example 5 strength tokens equal 1 reward token.) Children cannot trade tokens among themselves for favors. Having assigned each child his or her own color prevents this. If a child claims they have lost tokens or tokens come up "missing" do not replace them. Each child is responsible for the safekeeping of her or his stash.

Establish a value for a token, for example, $1.00, to determine how many tokens will be required for items. Do not convert tokens to cash for your children. The more specific the item your child is working toward obtaining, the better the motivation. Your child can prepare a short reward list (no more than 5 items) and maintain it, adding or subtracting the items they identified and ranking them in order of importance. While you as parents must approve the items on the list, it is not your responsibility to make the list for them. Based on the list, you determine the number of tokens it will take to acquire the object or activity. Some items may take a short while to obtain; others may take quite some time. This reinforces the concept of deferred gratification.

Rather than fifteen tokens = one game, ask your child to name a specific game on the reward list. If you are affixing tokens to a reward trip such as an amusement park, give your children sufficient notice so they have enough time to collect tokens. If they do not have the tokens, they cannot go on the reward trip. All excursions should not be aligned to the token system. Some trips are privilege trips just for being a part of the family (like a vacation). Not all rewards have a monetary value. Here is a mixture of sample rewards using your token economy.

Three tokens could be exchanged for

- an ice cream cone
- a pack of trading cards
- a one hour trip to the park
- a twenty minute bike ride or walk with mom or dad
- One hour playing the game of your child's choice

Ten to fifteen token selections might include

- Movie rentals of your child's choosing
- Roller skating, ice skating, bowling etc. for up to two hours
- A collectible or craft item up to about $10 value
- Two hour excursion or tour of zoo, gardens, park

Twenty tokens might "purchase"

- a night out with friends
- an extended curfew for a night out
- having a friend over to spend the night
- playing a round of golf with dad
- spending four hours shopping at the mall

Fifty tokens might be converted to

- a weekend away from home with some spending money
- an article of designer clothing
- dinner with a friend (or friends) at your child's favorite restaurant
- a weekend family outing such as a camping or fishing trip
- a ticket to a concert

You know best what your children want to have and what you are willing to let them have based on your economic and time constraints. Be sure to honor their wish list timely and strive to get the reward item to them within 24 hours of your child presenting the proper number of tokens for the items or activities they have identified. For excursions or family trips, setting a firm date for the event to take place sometime in the near future within 24 hours would work fine.

Allowances

You will have to decide if you want to give your children allowances in addition to the token system Allowances are a specified amount of money, usually given at regular intervals (most popular is weekly) and typically not tied to specific accomplishments or actions. While many parents believe that giving cash to a child in the form of an allowance helps them learn financial responsibility, how many parents can boast that their child never asks for additional money beyond the allowance? A token economy is equally effective in teaching the skills that lead to fiscal fitness and has the added benefit of developing a meaningful reward system so your children learn how to work for what they want. An informal study I did with families converting from cash allowances to tokens found that when children asked for money for specific reasons rather than having "money in their pockets" to use at will, it reduced the amount their child spent weekly by about 30%!

Chores

All children need well-defined chores and all children have some chores already. The subject of chores is broader than most children think about. When you talk with them about chores, remind them they already do a lot of chores every day. It is important that you not remind them to do their chores. This builds responsibility and promotes good character. At day's end simply note whether the daily chores were completed and reward or withhold reward as is appropriate. The same is true of weekly chores. Inspect and reward or not based on whether your child completed the chore on his own initiative, on time, and satisfactorily.

Two types of chores will be explored in this part of your Family Charter. Daily chores are mostly related to hygiene and health and the daily rhythm of the household; weekly chores are bigger and more time consuming. Daily chores might include activities such as

- Brush your teeth at bedtime without being prompted
- Place your dirty clothes in the clothes hamper
- Pick up toys and place in the toy chest

- Complete all homework by a specific time

- Set the dinner table by a specific time

- Feed the family pet by a specific time

- Go to bed on time without being reminded

Weekly chores might include

- Clean and dust your room before noon on Saturday

- Vacuum the carpet in the family room (child one) before 10:00 AM

- Vacuum the carpet in the hallway (child two) before 11:00 AM

- Do your own laundry and place it in your room no later than 6:00 PM

- Help parent take the sheets and towels to the laundry room

- Help parent fold the towels within ten minutes of the dryer buzzing

- Scrub the kitchen floor before 8:00 PM on Tuesday

Note that these chore examples are very specific and have a completion time and that they may include activities in your Character Card set. So what if a tub gets scrubbed twice in a day? Remember the distinction between chores and consequences. You assign chores; your child agrees to assign additional responsibilities and activities, often chore related, to herself when she chooses to break a published family rule. If you are using the reward system described above, make it clear that the reward is contingent upon completing the chore WITHOUT prompting. If you have to remind your child of the chore, the character building involved in taking responsibility for maintaining a harmonious home is lost.

The following is a brief list of generally agreed upon age-appropriate chores.

Ages nine months to two years

- Putting dirty clothes in hamper
- Handing groceries to mom to put away
- Picking up toys

Ages two - three

- Sorting items, like laundry
- Taking dishes and cups to the sink
- Setting out napkins and silverware neatly

Ages three - five

- Pick up clothes and toys
- Make the bed
- Set the table
- Clear dishes from the table
- Keep room organized
- Simple hygiene such as teeth brushing, hair combing, washing hands and face

Age six - nine

- Sweeping floors
- Dusting furniture
- Feeding pets
- Loading and unloading laundry (dry items) and folding small items